HOUSING ISSUES, LAWS AND PROGRAMS

MATERNAL, INFANT, AND EARLY CHILDHOOD HOME VISITING PROGRAM

BACKGROUND AND EVALUATION (WITH ACCOMPANYING CD-ROM)

HOUSING ISSUES, LAWS AND PROGRAMS

Additional books in this series can be found on Nova's website under the Series tab.

Additional e-books in this series can be found on Nova's website under the e-book tab.

HOUSING ISSUES, LAWS AND PROGRAMS

MATERNAL, INFANT, AND EARLY CHILDHOOD HOME VISITING PROGRAM

BACKGROUND AND EVALUATION (WITH ACCOMPANYING CD-ROM)

AARON L. STEWART
EDITOR

nova publishers
New York

Library of Congress Cataloging-in-Publication Data

ISBN: 978-1-63483-724-8

Published by Nova Science Publishers, Inc. † New York

CONTENTS

PREFACE

The Home Visiting Program is administered by the Health Resources and Services Administration (HRSA) in partnership with the Administration for Children and Families (ACF). Congress created the Maternal, Infant, and Early Childhood Home Visiting Program (Home Visiting Program) to support voluntary, evidence-based home visiting services for at-risk pregnant women and parents with young children up to kindergarten entry. The Home Visiting Program builds upon decades of scientific research showing that home visits by a nurse, social worker, early childhood educator, or other trained professional during pregnancy and in the first years of life improve the lives of children and families by preventing child abuse and neglect, supporting positive parenting, improving maternal and child health, and promoting child development and school readiness. Research also shows that evidence-based home visiting can provide a positive return on investment to society through savings in public expenditures on emergency room visits, child protective services, special education, as well as increased tax revenues from parents' earnings. This book examines the first findings from the Home Visiting Program.

In: Maternal, Infant, and Early Childhood … ISBN: 978-1-63483-724-8
Editor: Aaron L. Stewart

Chapter 1

THE MATERNAL, INFANT, AND EARLY CHILDHOOD HOME VISITING PROGRAM: PARTNERING WITH PARENTS TO HELP CHILDREN SUCCEED*

Health Resources and Services Administration

BACKGROUND

Congress created the Maternal, Infant, and Early Childhood Home Visiting Program (Home Visiting Program) to support voluntary, evidence-based home visiting services for at-risk pregnant women and parents with young children up to kindergarten entry. The Home Visiting Program builds upon decades of scientific research showing that home visits by a nurse, social worker, early childhood educator, or other trained professional during pregnancy and in the first years of life improve the lives of children and families by preventing child abuse and neglect, supporting positive parenting, improving maternal and child health, and promoting child development and school readiness. [1] Research also shows that evidence-based home visiting can provide a positive return on investment to society through savings in public expenditures on emergency room visits, child protective services,

* This is an edited, reformatted and augmented version of a program brief issued by the U.S. Department of Health and Human Services, 2015.

special education, as well as increased tax revenues from parents' earnings. [2, 3]

The Home Visiting Program is administered by the Health Resources and Services Administration (HRSA) in partnership with the Administration for Children and Families (ACF). States, territories, and tribal entities receive funding through the Home Visiting Program, and have the flexibility to tailor the program to serve the specific needs of their communities. By law, grantees must spend the majority of their Home Visiting Program grants to implement evidence-based home visiting models, with up to 25 percent of funding available to implement other promising approaches that will undergo rigorous evaluation. As of February 2015, 17 models have met the rigorous criteria for evidence of effectiveness and are considered evidence-based, and six grantees are implementing and evaluating nine different promising practices.

While there is some variation across evidence-based home visiting models (e.g., some programs serve expecting mothers while others serve families after the birth of a child), all programs share some common characteristics. In these voluntary programs, trained professionals meet regularly with expectant parents or families with young children in their homes, building strong, positive relationships with families who want and need support. Home visitors evaluate the families' needs and provide services tailored to those needs, such as:

- Teaching parenting skills and modeling effective techniques.
- Promoting early learning in the home with an emphasis on positive interactions between parents and children and the creation of a language-rich environment that stimulates early language development.
- Providing information and guidance on a wide range of topics including breastfeeding, safe sleep position, injury prevention, and nutrition.
- Conducting screenings and providing referrals to address postpartum depression, substance abuse, and family violence.
- Screening children for developmental delays and facilitating early diagnosis and intervention for autism and other developmental disabilities.
- Connecting families to other services and resources as appropriate.

Evidence-based home visiting programs help children and families get off to a better, healthier start.

EXPANDING TO SERVE MORE FAMILIES AND COMMUNITIES

In fiscal year 2014, states reported serving approximately 115,500 parents and children in 787 counties in all 50 states, the District of Columbia, and five territories through the Home Visiting Program (Figure 1). Nearly 60,000 (52 percent) of those participating were new enrollees. The number of children and parents served by the Home Visiting Program has tripled since 2012, and the number of home visits provided has quadrupled, with more than 1.4 million home visits provided over the past three years (Figure 2).

Recent Growth in the Home Visiting Program

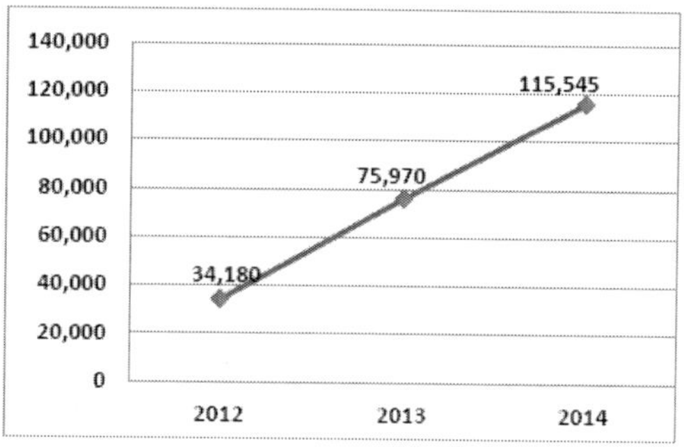

Figure 1. Number of Children and Parents Served. (2012-2014).

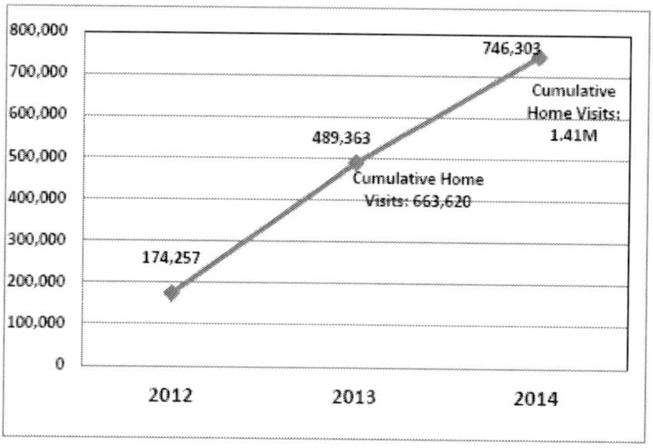

Figure 2. Number of Home Visits. (2012-2014).

States have also extended the reach of the Home Visiting Program into more communities:

- The total number of counties being served by the Home Visiting Program has more than doubled since the start of the program, reaching families in 787 counties as of February 2015, which represents 22 percent of all U.S. counties.
- The Home Visiting Program is reaching more communities with the highest need, serving families in approximately one-third of counties with high rates of infant mortality, children living in poverty, low-weight births, and teen births in 2014, compared to 18 percent of these counties in 2010.
- In 2014, the Home Visiting Program funded services in 30 percent of all urban counties, and 17 percent of all rural counties.
- In 2014, tribal grantees reported serving approximately 2,800 children and families as a result of the Tribal Home Visiting Program, and tribal grantees have provided nearly 18,000 home visits since the start of the program.

In order to effectively expand high-quality, evidence-based home visiting programs, many grantees spent the first two years of the program focusing much of their efforts on building infrastructure (e.g., establishing referral and data systems, conducting outreach to families, and recruiting and training a highly skilled home visiting workforce).

PROGRAM PARTICIPANTS

The Home Visiting Program serves many of our most vulnerable families. In 2014:

- 79 percent of participating families had household incomes at or below 100 percent of the federal poverty guidelines ($23,850 for a family four), and 48 percent were at or below 50 percent of those guidelines.
- 34 percent of adult program participants had less than a high school education, and 35 percent had a high school degree.

- 67 percent of program participants belonged to a racial or ethnic minority.
- Families served by the Home Visiting Program were at risk for poor family and child outcomes:
  - 27 percent of newly enrolled households included pregnant teens.
  - 20 percent of newly enrolled households reported a history of child abuse and maltreatment.
  - 12 percent of newly enrolled households reported substance abuse.

NOTABLE ACHIEVEMENTS

Home visiting services are already making a meaningful difference in the lives of vulnerable children and families.[1] Some examples of this progress include:

Developmental Delay: Less than 50 percent of young children with developmental or behavioral disabilities—such as autism, attention-deficit/hyperactivity disorder, or delays in language—are identified before they start school. [4] Early identification has been shown to improve the developmental trajectories of children with such delays or a developmental disability. In 2014, 14 grantees (AL, AZ, CA, CO, CT, ID, IL, KS, LA, MS, ND, NE, NM, TN) reported screening rates of at least 75 percent, more than twice the national average of 31 percent in 2011-2012. [5, 6]

- *New Mexico*: At six months after enrollment or birth, 90 percent of children in the Home Visiting Program were screened for developmental delay. In comparison, the state-wide screening rate among children aged 10 months to five years in 2011-2012 was 38 percent. [5]
- *Illinois:* 87 percent of enrolled children aged 12 months were screened for developmental delay. In 2011-2012, the state-wide screening rate among children aged 10 months to five years was 34 percent. [5]
- *Alabama:* 83 percent of enrolled children were screened for developmental delay within six months of enrollment. The state-wide screening rate was 25 percent in 2011-2012. [5]

Intimate Partner Violence (IPV): More than one-third of women report having experienced rape, physical violence, and/or stalking by an intimate partner at some point in their lifetime while nearly six percent report experiencing IPV in the past 12 months. [7] In addition to injuries, IPV is associated with adverse physical and mental health outcomes, and exposure of children to IPV can lead to health and behavioral problems, such as anxiety and depression. [8, 9 10] Despite these consequences, screening for IPV in many health care settings remains low, with only three percent to 41 percent of physicians reporting regularly screening for IPV. [11, 12] In 2014, 12 grantees (AK, AS, DE, IL, KY, LA, MI, NE, NV, SD, TN, VT) reported screening rates of at least 95 percent.

- *Tennessee:* More than 98 percent of enrolled mothers were screened for IPV at enrollment.
- *South Dakota:* More than 97 percent of enrolled pregnant women were screened for IPV within 36 weeks of pregnancy.
- *Indiana:* Nearly 95 percent of enrolled women were screened for IPV at enrollment.

Well-Child Visits: Well-child visits provide important opportunities for health care providers to evaluate a child's physical, emotional, and social development, as well as provide preventive care.

- *Colorado*: More than 99 percent of enrolled children had at least one well-child visit by six months of age.
- *Minnesota*: More than 99 percent of enrolled children had at least half of the recommended well-child visits.[2]
- *Pennsylvania:* 99 percent of enrolled children received the recommended number of well-child visits.[3]

Maternal Depression: When left untreated, maternal depression has been associated with adverse birth outcomes, poor mother-child bonding, and negative parenting behaviors, [13, 14, 15] which can impair the development, health, and safety of young children. [16, 17, 18] Yet, it has been estimated that less than half of primary care physicians regularly screen for maternal depression. [19, 20] In 2014, seven grantees (AZ, DE, IL, IN, ND, NY, SD) reported screening rates of at least 95 percent.

- *Arizona*: More than 99 percent of new mothers were screened for maternal depression within the first six months postpartum.
- *New York*: More than 95 percent of enrolled pregnant women were screened for maternal depression.
- *Wisconsin*: Nearly 95 percent of new mothers were screened for maternal depression within 60 days postpartum.

In addition to these services, home visitors support families by providing needed referrals and connections to services. For example, when a home visitor identifies that a child has a developmental delay, he or she will facilitate additional diagnostic testing and help the family access appropriate early intervention services.

TRIBAL HOME VISITING PROGRAM

The Tribal Home Visiting Program, administered by ACF, has awarded 25 grants to tribes, consortia of tribes, tribal organizations, and urban Indian organizations to develop, implement, and evaluate home visiting programs. The program is designed to develop and strengthen tribal capacity to support and promote the health and well-being of American Indian and Alaska Native families, expand the evidence base around home visiting in tribal communities, and support and strengthen cooperation and linkages between programs that serve Native children and their families.

Due to the limited evidence base on effective home visiting in tribal communities, Tribal Home Visiting grantees may adopt home visiting models that are either evidence-based or considered a promising approach. Model selection is designed to be a collaborative and community-driven process based on community needs. Because most home visiting models selected by grantees are designed for non-Native populations, many grantees have enhanced or adapted models to fit culture and context. Adaptations and enhancements include hiring culturally competent staff from the community, incorporating traditional parenting practices, and involving cultural leaders and elders as well as model developers throughout the program development and implementation process. In 2014, tribal grantees reported serving about 2,800 children and families as a result of the Tribal Home Visiting Program, and tribal grantees have provided nearly 18,000 home visits since the start of the program. For more information on the Tribal Home Visiting Program visit http://www.acf.hhs.gov/programs/ecd/homevisiting.

RESEARCH AND EVALUATION

ACF, in collaboration with HRSA, is overseeing the Mother and Infant Home Visiting Program Evaluation (MIHOPE), a large-scale, random assignment evaluation of the effectiveness of the Home Visiting Program. Using scientifically rigorous research methods, MIHOPE will estimate the effects of home visiting on a wide range of outcomes, study the variation in how programs are implemented, and conduct a cost analysis. The national evaluation will examine what components of home visiting programs work, for whom, and why, to provide all programs and models with information they can use to promote even greater positive outcomes for families. Study enrollment and data collection began in October 2012 and will continue through September 2015. As of December 2014, 12 states and 88 local programs are participating in the evaluation, and more than 3,700 families are enrolled (with up to 4,300 expected to participate overall).

In February 2015, HHS delivered the report to Congress on MIHOPE. This report presents the first findings from the study, and includes an analysis of the states' needs assessments, as well as baseline characteristics of families, staff, local programs, and models participating in the study.

The report shows that women enrolled in the evaluation face risks of adverse outcomes for themselves and their children, with:

- 34 percent having symptoms of depression, and approximately 20 percent having health problems that limited their activities.
- 33 percent reporting binge drinking or using illegal drugs before pregnancy.
- 35 percent having smoked in the past two years.
- 10 percent having been a victim of physical intimate partner violence in the past year.

The report found that local programs' infrastructure is aligned with Home Visiting Program expectations and designed to support quality service delivery for these families:

- Home visitors are well trained, especially in child development and parenting support, with most home visitors reporting that they are trained to help families across the full range of outcome areas specified in legislation.
- 66 percent of local programs have formal referral agreements.
- 73 percent have expert consultants available.
- 84 percent had some continuous quality improvement activities in the past year.

In addition, the report found that, prior to creation of the Home Visiting Program, home visiting programs were an important resource throughout the country, but many communities did not use evidence-based models or had unmet home visiting needs. In response, states planned to spend Home Visiting Program funds in communities that, compared with states' overall averages, had higher rates of poverty, poor birth outcomes, and child maltreatment. States' plans also pointed to an increase in use of evidence-based models, with funds used to support a combination of national models with evidence of effectiveness. Final reports on impacts, implementation, and cost effectiveness will be available in 2018.

For more information on the Home Visiting Program, visit http://www.mchb.hrsa.gov/programs/homevisiting.

REFERENCES

[1] U.S. Department of Health and Human Services, Administration for Children and Families, Home Visiting Evidence of Effectiveness (HomVEE). Available at : http://homvee.acf.hhs.gov/.

[2] Karoly, L, et al. (2005). Early Childhood Interventions: Proven Results, Future Promise. RAND Corporation. Santa Monica, California. Available at: http://www.rand.org/pubs/monographs/MG341.html

[3] Washington State Institute of Public Policy. Benefit-Cost Results. Available at: http://www.wsipp.wa.gov/BenefitCost

[4] U.S. Department of Education, Office of Special Education Programs, Data Analysis System (DANS), Part C Child Count, 1997–2006, from http://www.ideadata.org/PartCChildCount.asp (Accessed December 7, 2007).

[5] Child and Adolescent Health Measurement Initiative. Data Resource Center. Available at: http://www.childhealthdata.org. (Accessed December 31, 2014).

[6] American Academy of Pediatrics, Council on Children With Disabilities, Section on Developmental and Behavioral Pediatrics, Bright Futures Steering Committee, and Medical Home Initiatives for Children With Special Needs. (2006). Identifying Infants and Young Children with Developmental Disorder in the Medical Home: An Algorithm for Developmental Surveillance and Screening. [Published correction appears in Pediatrics. 2006;118(4):1808–1809]. *Pediatrics*. 118(1): 405–420.

[7] U.S. Department of Health and Human Services, Centers for Disease Control and Prevention. (2010). National Intimate Partner and Sexual Violence Survey: 2010 Summary Report. Available at: http://www.cdc.gov/violenceprevention/nisvs/summary reports.html. (Accessed December 16, 2014).

[8] Lamers-Winkelman, F, et al. (2012). Children's Physical Health Complaints After Exposure to Intimate Partner Violence. *British Journal of Health Psychology*. 17(4): 771-84.

[9] Yates, T, et. al. (2003). Exposure to Partner Violence and Child Behavior Problems: A Prospective Study Controlling for Child Physical Abuse and Neglect, Child Cognitive Ability, Socioeconomic Status and Life Stress. *Development and Psychopathology*. 15(1): 199-218.

[10] Russell, D, et. al. (2010). Witnessing Domestic Violence in Childhood as An Independent Risk Factor for Depressive Symptoms in Young Adulthood. *Child Abuse and Neglect*. 34(6): 448-453.

[11] De Boinville, M. (2013) ASPE Policy Brief: Screening for Domestic Violence in Health Care Settings. Available: http://aspe.hhs.gov/hsp/13/dv/pb screeningdomestic.cfm (Accessed January 8, 2015).

[12] Stayton, C, and Duncan, M. (2005). Mutable Influences on Intimate Partner Abuse in Health Care Settings: A Synthesis of the Literature. Trauma, Violence, and Abuse. 6(4). Available: http://tva.sagepub.com.ezproxyhhs.nihlibrary.nih.gov/content/6/4/271.full.pdf+html (Accessed October 30, 2012).

[13] Field, T. (2010). Postpartum Depression Effects on Early Interactions, Parenting, and Safety Practices: A Review. *Journal of Infant Behavioral Development*. 33: 1–6.

[14] Paulson, J, et. al. (2006). Individual and Combined Effects of Postpartum Depression in Mothers and Fathers on Parenting Behavior. *Pediatrics*. 118(2): 659- 668.
[15] Henderson, J, et. al. (2003). Impact of Postnatal Depression on Breastfeeding Duration. *Birth*. 30(3): 175-180.
[16] Whitaker, R, et. al. (2006). Maternal Mental Health, Substance Use, and Domestic Violence in the Year after Delivery and Subsequent Behavior Problems in Children at Age Three Years. *Archives of General Psychiatry*. 63(5): 551-560.
[17] Kavanaugh, M, et. al. (2006). Maternal Depressive Symptoms Are Adversely Associated with Prevention Practices and Parenting Behaviors for Preschool Children. *Ambulatory Pediatrics*. 6(1): 32-37.
[18] Sills, M, et. al. (2007). Association between Parental Depression and Children's Health Care Use. *Pediatrics*. 119(4): 829-836.
[19] LaRocco-Cockburn A, et. al. (2003). Depression Screening Attitudes and Practices Among Obstetrician-Gynecologists. *Obstetrics & Gynecology*. 101: 892-8.
[20] Seehusen, L, et.al (2005). Are Family Physicians Appropriately Screening for Postpartum Depression? *Journal of the American Board of Family Practice*. 18: 104–112.

End Notes

[1] The 56 Home Visiting Program grantees measure some aspect of screening for developmental delays, intimate partner violence, maternal depression and whether children receive well-child care. Since grantees have the flexibility to develop performance measures that are meaningful to their specific programs and local community needs, the benchmarks are measured in a number of ways.

[2] Adherence rate according to the Minnesota Child and Teen Check-up schedule.

[3] Adherence rate according to Pennsylvania Early and Periodic Screening, Diagnosis, and Treatment (EPSDT) Program.

In: Maternal, Infant, and Early Childhood … ISBN: 978-1-63483-724-8
Editor: Aaron L. Stewart

Chapter 2

THE MOTHER AND INFANT HOME VISITING PROGRAM EVALUATION: EARLY FINDINGS ON THE MATERNAL, INFANT, AND EARLY CHILDHOOD HOME VISITING PROGRAM*

Charles Michalopoulos, Helen Lee, Anne Duggan, Erika Lundquist, Ada Tso, Sarah Shea Crowne, Lori Burrell, Jennifer Somers, Jill H. Filene and Virginia Knox

OVERVIEW

Children from low-income families often have poor social, emotional, cognitive, behavioral, and health outcomes. One approach that has helped parents and their young children is home visiting, which provides information, resources, and support to expectant parents and families with young children. The Patient Protection and Affordable Care Act greatly expanded the availability of home visiting when it amended Title V of the Social Security Act to create the federal Maternal, Infant, and Early Childhood Home Visiting Program (MIECHV or the Home Visiting Program). In doing so, it allocated

---

* This is an edited, reformatted and augmented version of a report to Congress, OPRE Report 2015-11, issued by Office of Planning, Research and Evaluation, Administration for Children and Families, U.S. Department of Health and Human Services, January 2015.

$1.5 billion from fiscal year 2010 to fiscal year 2014 to states, territories, and tribal entities to fund home visiting programs. The Protecting Access to Medicare Act of 2014 provided an additional $400 million through the middle of fiscal year 2015. MIECHV required states to make a priority of services for at-risk families in order to improve a broad range of outcomes related to parental and child health and well-being, parenting, economic self-sufficiency, and intimate partner violence. It also required states to spend most funds on national models that met rigorous criteria for evidence of effectiveness defined by the Department of Health and Human Services (HHS).

This report presents the first findings from the Mother and Infant Home Visiting Program Evaluation (MIHOPE), the legislatively mandated national evaluation of MIECHV. Sponsored by the Administration for Children and Families and the Health Resources and Services Administration within HHS, MIHOPE is studying MIECHV in its early years. The study is being conducted for HHS by MDRC in partnership with James Bell Associates, Johns Hopkins University, Mathematica Policy Research, the University of Georgia, and Columbia University. Key findings in this report include:

- **States used initial MIECHV funds primarily to expand the use of four evidence-based home visiting models in at-risk communities.** The national home visiting models most frequently chosen by states for MIECHV funding were Early Head Start -Home Based Program Option, Healthy Families America, Nurse-Family Partnership, and Parents as Teachers. As intended, states targeted counties with high rates of poverty, child maltreatment, and premature birth, among other indicators of risk.
- **As intended, MIECHV-funded programs serve a group of mothers with many needs.** When they entered the study, more than 30 percent of women had symptoms of depression, almost 20 percent had health problems that limited their activities, 92 percent were receiving some form of public assistance, more than three-quarters had no more than a high school diploma, and a tenth reported being the victim of intimate partner violence.
- **MIECHV-funded programs are designed to help parents support the healthy development of infants and toddlers and overcome the problems low-income families face.** MIECHV encouraged some local programs to broaden the outcomes they focused on, and home visitors reported that they were generally well trained and supported in working with families to address a wide range of outcomes. Local

programs also reported having the management information systems and infrastructure they needed to implement programs effectively.

This report provides a foundation for understanding the implementation and impacts of MIECHV-funded home visiting programs. Later reports will explore the local and national implementation of those programs, and their effects on families with young children.

EXECUTIVE SUMMARY

Children from low-income families often suffer from poor social, emotional, cognitive, health, and behavioral outcomes.[1] Children develop fastest in their earliest years, and developing early skills and abilities lays the foundation for future success in school and life.[2] For that reason, the most cost-effective time to intervene may be early in a child's life.[3] One important approach that has helped parents and their young children is home visiting, which provides individually tailored information, resources, and support to expectant parents and families with young children.

Home visiting aims to support the healthy development of infants and toddlers and help low-income families overcome the problems they face. In general, it consists of three types of activities: assessment of family needs, parent education and support, and referral to and coordination with needed services. Home visitors use a variety of strategies to provide support and education to families, including setting goals with caregivers and creating plans for meeting those goals, helping caregivers resolve problems, helping parents and children build better relationships, intervening during crises, providing information on children's developmental stages and feedback on parenting, working to strengthen families' support networks, supporting and coordinating referrals to additional community resources, and providing emotional support, written information, or other materials.

The Patient Protection and Affordable Care Act greatly expanded the availability of home visiting in the United States when it amended Title V of the Social Security Act to create the federal Maternal, Infant, and Early Childhood Home Visiting Program (MIECHV or the Home Visiting Program). In doing so, it allocated $1.5 billion to states, territories, and tribal entities (which include tribes, tribal organizations, and urban Indian organizations) to fund home visiting from federal fiscal year (FY) 2010 through the middle of FY 2015.[4] The legislation also required an evaluation of MIECHV in its early years along with a report to Congress due by March 31, 2015. To fulfill these requirements, this report presents the first findings from the Mother and Infant Home Visiting Program Evaluation (MIHOPE). MIHOPE was launched in 2011 by the Administration for Children and Families and the Health Resources and Services Administration within the Department of Health and Human Services (HHS). The study is being conducted for HHS by MDRC in partnership with James Bell Associates, Johns Hopkins University, Mathematica Policy Research, the University of Georgia, and Columbia University.

The legislation required the evaluation to include four components:

- **Analysis of needs assessments.** The legislation required states and territories to assess the needs of local communities in order to determine where home visiting resources should be spent. The legislation required the evaluation to provide an analysis, on a state-by-state basis, of the results of the needs assessments, including indicators of maternal and prenatal health and infant health and mortality, and state actions in response to the assessments.
- **Effectiveness study.** The evaluation will assess the effect of early-childhood home visiting programs on child and parent outcomes, including health, child development, parenting skills, school readiness and academic achievement, crime or domestic violence, and family economic self-sufficiency.[5]
- **Subgroup analysis.** The evaluation will assess the effectiveness of the programs on different populations, including the extent to which the ability of the programs to improve participant outcomes varies across programs and populations.
- **Analysis of effects on the health care system.** The evaluation will assess whether the activities conducted by such programs, if expanded to a broad scale, have the potential to improve health care practices, eliminate health disparities, improve health care quality and efficiency, and reduce costs.

The current report presents MIHOPE's findings to date. These include information on the needs identified by states and their plans for using MIECHV funds to meet those needs, a description of where the study is being conducted, some information on the families in the study, and a discussion of whether plans for local home visiting programs reflect the requirements of MIECHV.

Home Visiting Models Studied in MIHOPE

MIHOPE is studying four national evidence-based models that, at the start of the study, were supported with MIECHV funds in 10 or more states.[6] These are Early Head Start-Home Based Program Option, Healthy Families America, Nurse-Family Partnership, and Parents as Teachers.

In general, home visiting programs work with expectant mothers and families with young children to do three things: (1) assess family needs, (2) educate and support parents, and (3) help families gain access to services, all with the goal of improving outcomes for families throughout their children's early years and beyond. Although the four national models follow this basic framework, they differ in some important ways.

- **Goals.** All of the models try to improve child health and development, but some have historically focused more on preventing child maltreatment, others on improving maternal and child health, and others on positive parenting or school readiness.
- **Target population and age at enrollment.** The models aim to serve at-risk families, such as those with low incomes. However, each focuses on different types of risk. Nurse-Family Partnership targets first-time mothers, Healthy Families America focuses on families at risk of child maltreatment or with behavioral health issues, Early Head Start seeks to serve a broad group of low-income families, and Parents as Teachers has no specific eligibility requirements at the national level. All four models can enroll women when they are pregnant or when they have newborns, although Early Head Start and Parents as Teachers also enroll families with toddlers.
- **Home visitor qualifications.** The four national models require different qualifications of their home visitors. Nurse-Family Partnership home visitors must be registered nurses, Early Head Start requires home visitors to have knowledge and experience in child development, Parents as Teachers requires home visitors to have at least a high school credential, and Healthy Families America does not require home visitors to have a specific educational background.

MIHOPE Study Design

MIHOPE plans to enroll more than 4,000 families through 88 local home visiting programs that are operating one of the four national evidence-based models in 12 states. The study is large enough to provide reliable information about MIECHV-funded programs' effects on the range of outcomes identified in the legislation and to provide information on the characteristics of more effective local programs. To generate the most credible estimates of those effects, families are being assigned at random to either a MIECHV-funded home visiting program or to a control group that will be referred to other appropriate services in the community.

Analysis of State Needs Assessments

To receive MIECHV funding, states were required to identify the quality and capacity of existing home visiting programs and to collect information on community characteristics to determine where MIECHV funds would be best spent. With that information in hand, they developed plans for spending those funds that covered where funds would be used, for which evidence-based models, and to target which families. The legislation required MIHOPE to analyze those needs assessments and state plans. Among the findings of that analysis are:

- **States chose high-needs communities for MIECHV funds.** As intended by the legislation, states generally proposed using MIECHV funds in counties with high rates of risk indicators. For example, most states targeted communities with high poverty and unemployment rates and high rates of premature births.
- **Home visiting services were extensive prior to MIECHV.** States identified more than 5,000 local home visiting programs operating prior to MIECHV. The most widely disseminated models were the four being studied in MIHOPE, but almost half of local home visiting programs used models that were not evidence-based according to HHS's criteria.
- **MIECHV encouraged states to expand the use of evidence-based home visiting models.** In their initial plans for using MIECHV funds, states proposed to support primarily the four national models being studied in MIHOPE. In interviews for MIHOPE, state administrators

confirmed that MIECHV encouraged them to expand the reach of evidence-based home visiting. As of their FY 2011 plans, 40 states planned to use MIECHV to support Nurse-Family Partnership programs, 39 for Healthy Families America programs, 29 for Parents as Teachers programs, and 17 for Early Head Start programs.

States and Local Programs Chosen for MIHOPE

As noted earlier, MIHOPE includes 88 MIECHV-funded local home visiting programs in 12 states. Since initial state plans indicated that MIECHV would support more than 500 such programs, the study had to choose which states and local programs to include.

MIHOPE selected states using several criteria:

- **They were using MIECHV funds to expand at least two of the four evidence-based models.** This would help the study distinguish between the influence of a particular state and the influence of a particular program model.
- **They were planning to support five or more eligible local programs.** Such states were considered a higher priority because they would help achieve the study's goal of choosing about 85 local programs from 12 states.
- **Collectively, they represented four geographic clusters.** These clusters corresponded to the Northeast, South, Midwest, and Mountain and West.

These criteria resulted in 12 states being selected for the study: California, Georgia, Illinois, Iowa, Kansas, Michigan, Nevada, New Jersey, Pennsylvania, South Carolina, Washington, and Wisconsin.

Within these states, MIHOPE selected local home visiting programs if they met the following criteria:

- They operated one of the four national evidence-based models.
- They had been in operation for two or more years and were thus past initial start-up challenges.
- They had enough demand for services that they could enroll at least 40 families for the study while allowing for the ethical creation of a control group.

- They helped provide an approximately equal distribution of local programs across the four national models. The local programs participating in MIHOPE include 19 operating Early Head Start, 26 operating Healthy Families America, 22 operating Nurse-Family Partnership, and 21 operating Parents as Teachers.

Family Characteristics

This section presents information on MIHOPE families using surveys of women conducted as they entered the study. Because sample recruitment continues, the findings are based on about a third of the families who will eventually be enrolled in the study. The characteristics of these families were shaped by the requirements of both the national models and of MIECHV. In particular, the legislation required states to give priority to families headed by parents who had served in the Armed Forces and to high-risk groups, including low-income, pregnant women under age 21; families with a history of child abuse or substance abuse; tobacco users; families with children who have low academic achievement; and children with developmental delays. In general, the national models aim to serve families with similar risk factors, although Nurse-Family Partnership is limited to women early in their first pregnancies, while Healthy Families America targets families at risk for child maltreatment or other negative childhood experiences.

The MIHOPE sample is young, with an average maternal age of 23 at the time of enrollment. Nearly 70 percent were pregnant, with about 43 percent in the legislation's priority population of pregnant women under age 21. The sample is also racially and ethnically diverse, with most mothers being Hispanic (34 percent), non-Hispanic white (25 percent), or non-Hispanic black (31 percent).

The information on families also provides insights into the risks and challenges faced by mothers and children in the outcome areas identified for improvement in the legislation.

- **Maternal health and well-being.** In some respects, women in MIHOPE exhibited healthy behavior and were in good health: 80 percent initiated prenatal care in the first trimester, and nearly 90 percent said they were in good or excellent health. At the same time, more than a third reported using tobacco and a third reported binge drinking in the three months before pregnancy or using illegal drugs in the months before pregnancy. Forty percent exhibited symptoms of depression or anxiety when they entered the study, and a tenth had been the victim of physical intimate partner violence in the past year.

- **Parenting.** To meet the goal of improving child health and development, all four national models emphasize positive parenting skills. Surveys of parents indicate some positive parenting practices before women entered the study, but also indicate some room for improvement. For example, nearly 80 percent of mothers had initiated breastfeeding and a similar number of pregnant women planned to breastfeed. However, only about half had at least 10 books in the home, which has been found to be an important predictor of children's ability to understand and use language and to think and understand.[7]
- **Family economic self-sufficiency.** Home visiting programs often target low-income families, and nearly all families in the study were receiving some government benefits intended for low-income families. In addition, 44 percent of mothers had not finished high school.
- **Child health and development.** Because children were very young or their mothers were pregnant when they entered the study, only a little is known about children's health and development at that time. Among the young children, about 10 percent were born prematurely and about 10 percent were born with low birth weights. Both rates are similar to national averages. Nearly every child had a usual source of health care, although about a tenth of children were not covered by health insurance.
- **Characteristics by national model.** As noted earlier, the four national models target somewhat different groups of families. In general, there were few differences in the types of families enrolled by the four models, although Nurse-Family Partnership programs enrolled only pregnant women while about half of the women enrolled by other MIHOPE programs were pregnant.

Characteristics of Home Visiting Programs

The familial risks described above underscore the challenges that home visiting programs face. This report describes how the four national models and the local home visiting programs participating in MIHOPE are planning and supporting the implementation of home visiting services. The information comes from interviews and surveys with the four national model developers, web-based surveys of 77 program managers around the time their programs entered the study, and web-based surveys with 377 home visitors around the same time.

Characteristics of Home Visiting Planned Services

This section describes whom programs intend to serve, what outcomes they intend to improve, what services they plan to deliver to achieve those improvements, and how they intend to staff programs to deliver services.

Intended Recipients

All four national models serve families at risk of poor child outcomes. All indicated to the MIHOPE team that they assume major responsibility for improving the outcomes of the child and all indicated that they assume at least some responsibility for the mother's outcomes. In general, local programs are consistent with their national models in this respect.

Intended Goals and Outcomes

When presented with a list of outcomes ranked as high priorities in the legislation that created MIECHV, all four national model developers assigned high priorities to five outcomes: promoting positive parenting behavior, preventing child abuse and neglect, fostering economic self-sufficiency, encouraging child preventive care, and promoting child development. However, the national model developers differed for other outcomes. Nurse-Family Partnership, for example, gave the highest priority to all of the outcomes, while Parents as Teachers placed a high priority on some but low priority on others. Despite differences among the national models, a majority of local program managers ranked each outcome highly. This may reflect the influence of MIECHV: some local programs claimed that MIECHV encouraged them to make a higher priority of outcomes mentioned in the authorizing legislation.

Intended Service Delivery

Home visits generally consist of information gathering, education and support, and referrals for needed services. Nearly all local programs reported that they required formal screening to identify maternal mental health issues and infant developmental delays, and about three-quarters required formal assessment of participants for maternal substance abuse, intimate partner violence, and parenting behavior. This is consistent with the requirements of the national models, which all required local programs to conduct developmental screenings but varied in their requirements for screening in other areas. Despite the widespread use of screening, many local programs lacked protocols for education and support in cases where screens detected problems. For example, when they entered MIHOPE, only about half of the local programs had protocols for responding to developmental delays and fewer than half had written protocols for the other problems that screens might detect, such as maternal substance use, intimate partner violence, or poor parenting behavior. Turning to referral policies, many local programs reported that home visitors were expected to help families gain access to necessary resources, which is consistent with national model requirements that home visitors monitor families' success in using referrals.

Regarding the approaches that home visitors use in their daily work with families, all four national models encouraged observation of parent-child interaction accompanied by both positive and constructive feedback, and all of the national models encouraged home visitors to use at least one supportive strategy such as goal setting, problem solving, or emotional support. However, only Early Head Start and Nurse-Family Partnership encouraged home visitors to demonstrate positive parenting practices, and Early Head Start, Healthy Families America, and Nurse-Family Partnership encouraged home visitors to direct parent-child activities. In contrast to their national models, most local programs across all national models reported that they encouraged the use of all of these techniques.

Implementation System

The implementation system is the link between intended and actual service delivery. The components of the implementation system discussed in this report include staff development, clinical support, administrative support, and system support.

Staff Development

In web-based surveys, most home visitors indicated that they were expected to help mothers across the range of outcomes described earlier. The vast majority of home visitors also reported they were adequately trained to help mothers in these areas, and that local programs provided useful strategies and tools to assist them in helping mothers.

Clinical Support

Because of the complex challenges seen in disadvantaged families, local programs may provide home visitors with access to expert advice from clinical consultants. Overall, about three-quarters of local programs reported that they did provide access to expert consultants, and the availability of expert consultants was relatively uniform across outcome domains.

Links to Community Resources

Home visiting programs must work with other organizations to identify eligible families and to connect them with needed services. Overall, two-thirds of local programs had formal referral agreements with organizations in their communities, although fewer than a quarter had formal referral agreements with health-related organizations.

Administrative Support

Nearly all local home visiting programs used management information systems for internal program monitoring. Most monitored the number of referrals into their programs and their retention rates, and most home visitors could use these systems to document what happened during home visits. As required under MIECHV, the majority of local programs had undertaken continuous quality improvement activities in the year prior to entering MIHOPE.[8]

Discussion

This report provides an early indication that MIECHV is being implemented in ways that support its intended goals. First, states developed plans to use MIECHV funds to expand evidence-based home visiting in at-risk communities. Reflecting those plans, local programs are serving a high-needs group of mothers, including some of the high-priority groups specified in the Affordable Care Act. Finally, MIECHV-funded programs appear to be designed to help families overcome the multiple and severe problems they face, and where there are gaps between families' needs and the services they provide, they appear to be paying attention to MIECHV goals and adjusting their priorities accordingly.

This report also sets the stage for future reports on the services delivered under MIECHV and the effects of the home visiting programs on family and child outcomes. It suggests that MIHOPE is well positioned to learn about the effects of home visiting for many of the high-priority groups identified in the authorizing legislation. It also suggests that MIHOPE can provide valuable information on several aspects of program implementation, including how local program implementation varies across the national models and how the quality of home visiting services varies with the priority that local programs and national models give to different outcomes.

SECTION 1. INTRODUCTION

Children from low-income families often suffer from poor social, emotional, cognitive, behavioral, and health outcomes.[9] Children develop fastest in their earliest years, and the skills and abilities they develop in those years help lay the foundation for future success in school and life.[10] For that reason, the most cost-effective time to intervene may be early in a child's life.[11] Since parents play a critical role in shaping children's early development, early interventions with parents have great potential to produce long-term benefits.[12]

One approach that has helped parents and their young children is home visiting, which provides individually tailored information, resources, and support to expectant parents and families with young children. Home visiting programs in the United States have their origins in the late nineteenth century, when charitable organizations used home visiting to try to reduce poverty by changing the behavior of the urban poor.[13] Home visiting later expanded to include such approaches as visits by public health nurses to promote infant and child health, Head Start home visiting to promote child development, and home-based family support to promote positive parenting and prevent child maltreatment.[14] The Patient Protection and Affordable Care Act greatly expanded the availability of home visiting in the United States when it amended Title V of the Social Security Act to create the federal Maternal, Infant, and Early Childhood Home Visiting Program (MIECHV or the Home Visiting Program) and allocated $1.5 billion to states, territories, and tribal entities (which include tribes, tribal organizations, and urban Indian organizations) to fund home visiting from federal fiscal year 2010 through the middle of fiscal year 2015.[15]

The legislation also required an evaluation of MIECHV in its early years, the Mother and Infant Home Visiting Program Evaluation (MIHOPE). MIHOPE was launched in 2011 by the Administration for Children and Families and the Health Resources and Services Administration within the

Department of Health and Human Services (HHS). The evaluation is being conducted for HHS by MDRC in partnership with James Bell Associates, Johns Hopkins University, Mathematica Policy Research, the University of Georgia, and Columbia University.

The overarching goals of MIHOPE are to learn whether families and children benefit from home visiting, and to investigate how states and local agencies implemented home visiting under MIECHV to improve family outcomes. In addressing these two issues, MIHOPE is also collecting a wealth of information to analyze which features of local home visiting programs increase their effectiveness. It is therefore designed to provide an unprecedented resource to help national, state, and local home visiting administrators develop and put into place effective home visiting programs.

This report presents the first findings from the study. The report's findings include:

- **States targeted at-risk communities for MIECHV funds.** The legislation required states and territories (hereafter referred to as states) to assess the needs of local communities in order to determine where home visiting resources should be spent. An analysis of those needs assessments reveals that home visiting programs were an important resource throughout the country prior to MIECHV, but that many communities did not use evidence-based models or had unmet home visiting needs. States proposed to spend MIECHV funds in communities that, compared with states' overall averages, had higher poverty rates, higher rates of poor birth outcomes, higher rates of child maltreatment, and worse rates for other indicators of disadvantage.
- **MIHOPE chose a diverse set of local home visiting programs.** As of May 2014, 12 states and 88 local home visiting programs had joined the study, including 19 Early Head Start-Home Based Program Option (also referred to as Early Head Start in this report), 26 Healthy Families America, 22 Nurse-Family Partnership, and 21 Parents as Teachers programs. Because larger programs were more likely to meet the study's sample requirements and rural programs tended to be smaller, over three-quarters of local programs included in MIHOPE operate in metropolitan counties.
- **Women enrolled in MIHOPE programs face many risks.** Because home visiting focuses on women with risk factors such as poverty or an environment conducive to child maltreatment, women in the

MIHOPE sample are at risk of adverse outcomes. They are generally quite young and poor, with limited education or work experience. They also face high levels of depression and high rates of intimate partner violence.

- **National home visiting models and local programs implementing those models vary in the outcomes they are trying to influence and in how they intend to provide services.** Although all national models studied in MIHOPE make a high priority of improving parenting, child health and development, and economic self-sufficiency, some place less emphasis on improving maternal health and health behaviors. Perhaps because MIECHV has asked states and local programs to improve these outcomes as well, when they entered the study most local home visiting programs said they emphasized the full range of outcomes, even outcomes that were not emphasized by their national models. In addition, most home visitors perceived that they were expected to help mothers across a wide range of outcomes and believed they were trained to do so.

MIECHV and MIHOPE

According to the authorizing legislation, MIECHV is intended to improve outcomes for families in at-risk communities, which includes those with concentrations of the following: poverty, crime, domestic violence, adverse birth outcomes such as premature birth and infant mortality, high school dropouts, substance abuse, unemployment, and child maltreatment. States are to give priority to individuals who are in the Armed Forces or who previously served, and to specific high-risk subgroups including low-income, pregnant women under age 21; families with a history of child abuse or substance abuse; tobacco users; families with children who have low academic achievement; and children with developmental delays.

The legislation that created MIECHV requires each state to use a majority of funds to support home visiting models with "evidence of effectiveness." To determine which national models fit into this category, HHS commissioned the Home Visiting Evidence of Effectiveness (HomVEE) review, which is being conducted by Mathematica Policy Research.[16] As of May 2014, HomVEE had found 14 models that met HHS's criteria for evidence of effectiveness, which means at least one study of at least moderate quality found statistically significant impacts in two or more of eight outcome domains, or at least two such studies found statistically significant impacts in the same domain.[17]

The legislation required the evaluation to include four components:

- **Analysis of needs assessments.** An analysis, on a state-by-state basis, of the results of the needs assessments, including indicators of maternal and prenatal health and infant health and mortality, and state actions in response to the assessments.
- **Effectiveness study.** An assessment of the effect of early childhood home visiting programs on child and parent outcomes.
- **Subgroup analysis.** An assessment of the effectiveness of the programs on different populations, including the extent to which the ability of the programs to improve participant outcomes varies across programs and populations.
- **Analysis of effects on the health care system.** An assessment of whether the activities conducted by such programs, if expanded to a broad scale, have the potential to improve health care practices, eliminate health disparities, improve health care quality and efficiency, and reduce costs.

MIHOPE is also collecting extensive information on how local programs are implemented, which will allow the evaluation to describe the home visiting services that are delivered under MIECHV, how those vary from place to place, and how variation in program implementation is linked to variation in program effects.

Research on Home Visiting Programs

Although there have been a number of previous studies of home visiting, syntheses of those studies have generally found modest benefits for families on average. But they have also found that effects have varied across studies.[18] This raises several issues that MIHOPE seeks to address.

- **Inconsistent effects.** Across program models and even within a given evidence-based model, effects have often varied for different groups of families. In addition, findings of effects for certain outcomes and subgroups have often not been replicated in later studies. MIHOPE is large enough to detect modest effects so that the field has clear evidence on the effects of evidence-based home visiting programs on the outcomes of interest.

- **Different outcomes tested in different studies.** One difficulty in interpreting home visiting research is that different studies have measured different outcomes. In part, this is because different program models target different domains, and studies of those models may have only focused on the targeted outcomes. In addition, different evaluators have looked at different measures within a given outcome domain. MIHOPE is designed to add to the existing body of knowledge about home visiting programs by collecting consistent information across all relevant outcome domains for all four models being studied.
- **Insufficient evidence of effectiveness in subgroups.** HomVEE found that many studies of home visiting programs did not include enough families to allow a precise analysis of subgroup effects, and those studies that have examined how effects varied by subgroup have often focused on different subgroups. This has led to thin evidence on some subgroups. MIHOPE is filling this gap by including enough families of sufficient diversity to help identify what works for different types of families.
- **Lack of information on program implementation.** Prior studies of human service programs have found that their implementation is associated with a number of factors such as program maturity and the detail and specificity of the intervention.[19] However, evaluations of home visiting programs have rarely collected detailed information on the services delivered. This makes it difficult to know whether weak impacts are due to problems of implementation or problems with the program model itself. MIHOPE is filling this gap by systematically examining how program features and implementation systems are associated with service delivery and impacts.
- **Program models that have changed over time.** Some of the evidence reviewed in HomVEE is as much as 40 years old, and most of the evidence-based models have changed over time to reflect growing knowledge about best practices. Thus, results from HomVEE might not reflect the effectiveness of those models as they are currently delivered.

The gap in knowledge on program implementation has recently been filled to some extent by the Administration for Children and Families through the

Supporting Evidence-Based Home Visiting to Prevent Child Maltreatment Initiative. That study of 17 agencies implementing home visiting across 15 states found substantial variation in fidelity among programs running the same national model.[20] The study found that among the important factors in delivering high-quality services were the strength of the home visitor-parent relationship, the clarity of a program's goals and measures of success, and the presence of an appropriate infrastructure for achieving desired goals. MIHOPE is designed to go the next step to investigate whether these and other features of home visiting programs lead to larger or broader effects for families and children.

MIHOPE Study Design

To provide reliable estimates of the effects of home visiting programs, families recruited into the study are being randomly assigned either to a MIECHV program or to a control group that will be referred to other appropriate services in the community.[21] In total, MIHOPE expects to include more than 4,000 families spread across 88 local programs that are operating one of four evidence-based models in 12 states. MIHOPE will thus provide precise estimates of the effects of home visiting on families, both for the full sample and for key subgroups of families. The large number of local programs will also provide the study with an opportunity to learn about the relationship between local program features and the impacts of home visiting on family and child outcomes.

Since it can be difficult to compare many outcomes across a broad range of children's ages, and because the majority of MIECHV-funded programs target women during pregnancy or shortly after childbirth, MIHOPE includes only families in which the mother is pregnant or the child is less than 6 months old when the family enrolls in the study.

The National Home Visiting Models Studied in MIHOPE

As will be discussed in Section 2, states' initial plans indicated they would use MIECHV primarily to support four national evidence-based models: Early Head Start, Healthy Families America, Nurse-Family Partnership, and Parents as Teachers. Because they were the only four national models chosen by 10 or more states in their initial plans, MIHOPE is studying only those four models. This section provides an overview of the four models.

In general, home visiting consists of three types of activities: assessment of family needs, parent education and support, and referral to and coordination with needed services. Home visitors use a variety of strategies to provide education and support to families, including setting goals with caregivers and creating plans for meeting those goals, helping caregivers resolve problems, helping parents and children build better relationships, intervening during crises, providing information on children's developmental stages and feedback on parenting, working to strengthen families' support networks, and providing emotional support, pamphlets, or other materials. Home visitors also use methods such as positive reinforcement, direct feedback, and motivational interviewing and reflection to encourage parents to change particular attitudes and behaviors. Finally, home visitors provide referrals to community health and human service resources based on each family's identified needs.

Although the four national models share these major components as well as the overall goal of improving outcomes for at-risk families and their young children, they differ in a number of important ways. Table 1.1 summarizes some important features of the four national models.

- **Program goals.** While all of the models try to improve child health and development in the broad sense, their specific goals differ. For example, Early Head Start provides comprehensive services that focus on the development of infants and toddlers, supporting parents in their roles as caregivers and teachers of their children and promoting school readiness. In addition to the goals of strengthening nurturing parent-child relationships, promoting healthy childhood growth and development, and enhancing family functioning, Healthy Families America has a particular emphasis on preventing child maltreatment. Nurse-Family Partnership has a strong emphasis on prevention and on the social determinants of health, particularly on improving birth outcomes through preventive health practices and improving child health and development. It also aims to improve mothers' economic self sufficiency and development. Parents as Teachers' focus is on supporting families to enhance parents' knowledge of early childhood development, improve parenting practices, help detect early signs of developmental delays and health issues, and promote children's school readiness and success.

- **Target population and age at enrollment.** Most of these models serve families they identify as being at risk of poor child outcomes, based on one or more family characteristics. Although the indicators used to identify families at risk differ among the models, most models target low-income families. Nurse-Family Partnership specifically targets women early in their first pregnancies, while Healthy Families America targets parents during any pregnancy or shortly after birth who face a variety of risk factors for child maltreatment or other negative childhood experiences (risk factors such as histories of trauma or intimate partner violence, behavioral health issues, and single parenthood). Parents as Teachers has historically served a broad array of families with children in its target age range. All of the models can enroll women when they are pregnant or when they have newborns, although Early Head Start and Parents as Teachers accept families whose youngest child is up to 3 years old and through kindergarten entry, respectively. This means that Early Head Start and Parents as Teachers enroll a much broader range of families than are being studied in MIHOPE, which includes only families with children under 6 months old.
- **Program intensity and duration.** The national models also vary somewhat in the frequency of home visits and the age at which they stop. Early Head Start has weekly home visits, while Healthy Families America and Nurse-Family Partnership offer weekly visits during critical periods (for example, shortly after birth) and Parents as Teachers specifies monthly or biweekly visits depending on families' needs. While Nurse-Family Partnership provides services through a child's second year, Early Head Start generally continues home visits through a child's third year, Healthy Families America can continue until a child is 5 years old, and Parents as Teachers varies by local program but can last until a child enters kindergarten.
- **Home visitor qualifications.** The national models have a wide range of standards for home visitor qualifications. For example, Nurse-Family Partnership requires that home visitors be registered nurses with a minimum of a bachelor's degree in nursing, but Healthy Families America recommends selecting home visitors based on a combination of personal characteristics (such as being nonjudgmental and compassionate), willingness to work in culturally diverse communities, experience working with families with multiple needs, and educational background. Early Head Start requires home visitors

to have experience in child development, early childhood education, and other areas,[22] while Parents as Teachers requires home visitors to have at least a high school credential (with a bachelor's degree recommended), plus two years of experience working with young children or parents.

- **Local variation.** Although not noted in the table, the national models vary in how much flexibility they allow local programs. For example, Nurse-Family Partnership has specific requirements regarding whom its programs can serve, the curricula that can be used, and the qualifications home visitors must have. In contrast, Early Head Start allows local programs flexibility in choosing curricula and setting the educational requirements of home visitors;[23] Healthy Families America allows considerable flexibility for local programs to decide target populations, curricula, and the educational backgrounds of home visitors (as long as they meet the other criteria described above); and Parents as Teachers provides local programs with a specific parenting curriculum but allows them flexibility in selecting target populations and eligibility criteria.

Questions Addressed by this Report

This report presents early evidence from MIHOPE to address the following questions:

- **Did states target the types of communities specified in the legislation that created MIECHV?** Section 2 answers this question, presenting an analysis of the needs assessments that states, territories, and the District of Columbia completed to obtain MIECHV funds and summarizing the types of communities that states identified as in need of home visiting.
- **Will the states and local home visiting programs chosen for MIHOPE provide reliable information on MIECHV nationally?** Section 3 explains the process for choosing states and local programs for the study, and describes those that were chosen.
- **Do MIECHV programs target the high-priority and high-needs families mentioned in the legislation?** Section 4 addresses this question, describing the families enrolled in MIHOPE through January 15, 2014 using data from surveys completed by study participants and observations of their home environments made by research team field interviewers.

Table 1.1. Key Components of the Planned Services of the Evidence-Based Home Visiting Programs in the Evaluation

Home Visiting Model	Program Goals	Target Population/ Age at Enrollment	Program Intensity/Duration	Home Visitor Qualifications
Early Head Start - Home Based Program Option	Enhance the development of very young children Promote healthy family functioning	The program targets low-income pregnant women and families with children birth to age 3, families at or below the federal poverty level, and children with disabilities who are eligible for Part C services under the Individuals with Disabilities Education Act in their state. Services can begin prenatally.	Weekly home visits for a minimum of 90 minutes Minimum of 48 home visits and 22 group socialization activities per year Services offered until the child is 3 years old (and older in some circumstances)	Home visitors must have knowledge and experience in child development and early childhood education; principles of child health, safety, and nutrition; adult learning principles; and family dynamics. Home visitors must effectively communicate with children and families with no or limited English proficiency directly or through an interpreter, and be familiar with the ethnic backgrounds of these families.

Home Visiting Model	Program Goals	Target Population/ Age at Enrollment	Program Intensity/Duration	Home Visitor Qualifications
Healthy Families America	Systematically reach out to parents to offer resources and support Cultivate the growth of nurturing, responsive parent-child relationships Promote healthy childhood growth and development Build the foundations for strong family functioning	The program targets parents facing challenges such as single parenthood, low income, childhood history of abuse or adverse experiences, current or prior behavioral health issues, or domestic violence. Individual programs select the specific characteristics of the target populations they plan to serve. Families are enrolled prenatally or within the first 3 months after a child's birth.	Home visits typically a minimum of 60 minutes Minimum of weekly home visits for the first 6 months after a child's birth; frequency of the visits after 6 months determined by local programs based on family risk factors Services beginning prenatally or at birth and continuing through the first 3 to 5 years of life	There are no specific educational requirements for home visitors. Home visitors should be selected based on personal characteristics and experience in working with families with multiple needs, experience working with or providing services to children and families, ability to establish trusting relationships, acceptance of individual differences, experience in working with culturally diverse communities, knowledge of infant and child development, and ability to maintain

Table 1.1. (Continued)

Home Visiting Model	Program Goals	Target Population/ Age at Enrollment	Program Intensity/Duration	Home Visitor Qualifications
				boundaries between personal and professional lives.
Nurse-Family Partnership	Improve prenatal health and outcomes Improve child health and development Improve families' economic self-sufficiency and maternal life-course development	The program targets first-time, low-income mothers and their children. The first home visit must occur no later than the end of week 28 of pregnancy. Programs are recommended to begin conducting visits in the 2nd trimester (14 to 16 weeks of gestation).	Home visits typically 60 to 75 minutes Weekly home visits for the 1st month after enrollment, then every other week until baby is born Weekly home visits for the first 6 weeks after the baby is born and then every other week until the baby is 20 months; last 4 visits monthly until the child is 2 years old Visit schedule potentially adjusted to meet client needs	Home visitors must be registered professional nurses with a minimum of a bachelor's degree in nursing.
Parents as Teachers	Provide parents with child development knowledge and parenting support	The program has no eligibility requirements for participants. Local programs select the specific characteristics of	Home visits recommended to last between 50 and 60 minutes	Parent educators must have high school diplomas or General Educational Development (GED)

Home Visiting Model	Program Goals	Target Population/ Age at Enrollment	Program Intensity/Duration	Home Visitor Qualifications
	Provide early detection of developmental delays and health issues Prevent child abuse and neglect Increase school readiness	their target populations, such as children with special needs, families at risk for child abuse, families with low incomes, teen parents, first-time parents, immigrant families, families with little literacy, or parents with mental health or substance abuse issues. Programs target enrollment prenatally or soon after birth.	Minimum of 10-12annual visits and 20-24 annual visits for higher-need families on a monthly, biweekly, or weekly basis Monthly group connections (meetings) offered Length and intensity of services determined by local programs, potentially lasting from pregnancy through kindergarten entry	certificates and a minimum of 2 years' previous supervised work experience with young children or parents. It is preferable for parent educators to have at least a 4-year degree in early childhood education or a related field or at least a 2-year degree or 60 college hours in early childhood education or a related field. Parent educators should have experience working with young children or parents.

SOURCES: Program model websites and the U.S. Department of Health and Human Services HomVEE website: http://homvee.acf.hhs.gov/ programs.aspx.

- **Do national models and the local programs that implement those models report goals and infrastructure consistent with the expectations of MIECHV?** Will variation in their approaches allow the study to determine which program features lead to larger benefits for families? Section 5 addresses these questions.

The final section summarizes the findings and discusses their implications for future MIHOPE reports.

SECTION 2. ANALYSIS OF THE STATE NEEDS ASSESSMENTS AND STATE PLANS

The legislation that created the Maternal, Infant, and Early Childhood Home Visiting Program (MIECHV) required states and territories (referred to as "states" in the remainder of this section) to assess which of their communities might need home visiting services because they had concentrations of premature birth, school dropouts, substance abuse, or other indicators.[24] States were also required to report on the quality and capacity of existing home visiting programs, including home visiting models already in use and the number of families they served, and to discuss any gaps or duplications in the services available in the identified communities. To receive MIECHV funds, states were also required to create plans that indicated in which communities the funds would be used and the home visiting models that would be supported with them.

This section summarizes information from the needs assessments and state plans, including (1) the extent to which home visiting services were available prior to MIECHV, (2) the communities identified by states as in need of home visiting, and (3) the evidence-based models and promising approaches states planned to support through MIECHV. The section also summarizes information, gathered from interviews with MIECHV administrators in the states participating in the Mother and Infant Home Visiting Program Evaluation (MIHOPE), about how the needs assessments were developed and used in determining where and how to spend MIECHV funds.

Main Findings

- **All states had home visiting services prior to MIECHV.** The typical state identified eight home visiting program models in operation. States reported using many different approaches to home visiting, and nearly half of the local home visiting programs identified by states were not using "evidence-based" models, defined as ones that met criteria for effectiveness designed by the Department of Health and Human Services (HHS).[25]
- **States also found many areas with unmet needs and focused MIECHV funds on those areas.** Within a state, communities targeted for MIECHV funding generally had higher rates of premature birth, poverty, unemployment, and child maltreatment than the state overall. Home visiting services were already available in the vast majority of these communities, but they were not serving all families in need and were not necessarily operating in the specific neighborhoods where the newly expanded evidence-based services would be provided.
- **MIECHV encouraged states to support evidence-based home visiting.** The legislation required states to spend a majority of MIECHV funds on "evidence-based" models. Although many preexisting home visiting programs implemented models that did not meet those criteria, states planned to use MIECHV funds primarily to support evidence-based models. The most frequently proposed models in the states' initial plans were the four models included in MIHOPE: Nurse-Family Partnership, Healthy Families America, Parents as Teachers, and Early Head Start-Home Based Program Option. Most states used MIECHV funds to expand evidence-based models already in operation in the state rather than to fund new models.
- **MIECHV administrators used a complex process to choose where to spend funds.** Interviews with state MIECHV administrators indicated that the needs assessment process helped them identify high-risk communities, but was not the only source of information used in making decisions. For example, some states balanced need with the ability of local areas to adequately implement home visiting services, based on state assessments of local infrastructure and capabilities.

Home Visiting Services Available Prior to MIECHV

To help states determine which areas were most in need of home visiting services, the legislation required each state to describe the home visiting programs that existed there prior to MIECHV and the numbers and types of individuals and families served by these programs. Each state was also asked to describe the gaps in home visiting services there and the extent to which existing programs were meeting the needs of eligible families. Appendix A provides information about the home visiting services described by states in their needs assessments.

With one month to complete their needs assessments, states varied in how comprehensively they were able to respond to the requests for information. States also varied in the information they provided about existing home visiting services and in what they considered to be home visiting programs. Because the Health Resources and Services Administration (HRSA) and the Administration for Children and Families did not specify what should be considered a "program," some states named home visiting models while others named the organizations implementing the programs. Given the variation in what states identified as "programs," this report refers to "state-identified programs" when discussing the programs that states reported in their needs assessments. The average state reported eight such programs operating prior to MIECHV. State-identified programs varied widely in their geographic coverage, with some serving large portions of a state and others serving a portion of a county. Many states did not provide the requested information for all their state-identified programs; in particular, only a minority of states provided detailed information on the demographic characteristics of the families served by the programs they identified. One reason for this was that information was often limited to what was shared by the organizations operating these programs. Finally, it is important to remember that because home visiting services can operate across a range of state, county, and private agencies, the administrators charged with gathering information may not have been aware of every home visiting program operating in their states.

Information on home visiting models identified by two or more states is summarized in Table 2.1, while other programs are shown in Appendix B. Table 2.1 also divides home visiting models into those that were found to be evidence-based by the HomVEE review as of 2010 and those that were not. In total, 19 models were reported as being implemented by two or more states, although the use of some models may be underreported to the extent that states missed some programs in their needs assessments or neglected to specify the model used by some programs.

Table 2.1. Home Visiting Models Used by State-Identified Programs Operating Prior to MIECHV

Model	Number of States	Number of Counties[a]
Evidence-based as of 2010		
Early Head Start - Home Based Program Option	50	933
Family Check-Up	0	0
Healthy Families America	33	592
Healthy Steps	1	3
Home Instruction for Parents of Preschool Youngsters	17	137
Nurse-Family Partnership	36	367
Parents as Teachers	48	785
Non-evidence-based as of 2010		
Early Steps to School Success	5	85
Even Start: Home Visiting	7	66
Family Connections	2	16
Head Start: Home-Based	22	329
Healthy Start: Home Visiting	17	176
Homebuilders Program	4	11
Maternal Infant Health Outreach Worker	3	13
Nurturing Parenting Programs	7	15
Parent-Child Home Program	11	64
Positive Parenting Program	2	3
Resource Mothers Program	3	72
SafeCare[b]	4	107
Other[c]	50	1,789

Source: 2010 MIECHV state needs assessments. For a few states, information on state-identified programs was supplemented with information from the state plans or first round of competitive grant applications.

Notes: This table includes all models that had been designated as evidence-based by the HomVEE project as of 2010, in time for states to include them in their FY 2010 and FY 2011 state plans, and models that were reported in use by more than one state.

In this table, "state" is used as shorthand for states, territories, and the District of Columbia.

[a] The number of counties offering each model is an estimate. For models that were reported to be implemented by multiple programs in a state, this table assumes that the number of counties offering the model in a state is equal to the largest number of counties served by the model by one program. This table also assumes that for organizations offering multiple models, every county served by the organization has at least one family receiving each of the models the organization offers.

[b] SafeCare Augmented, an adaptation of SafeCare, has been designated as evidence-based since 2010. It is unclear how many states and counties in this table used this adaptation.

[c] "Other" refers to programs that either used a model reported by only one state or did not specify a model in the needs assessments. A full list of these is in Table B.1.

Table 2.1 shows that the most frequently implemented models prior to MIECHV were Early Head Start, operating in 50 states and 933 counties; Parents as Teachers, in 48 states and 785 counties; Nurse-Family Partnership, in 36 states and 367 counties; and Healthy Families America, in 33 states and 592 counties. Other models reported to be operating in a large number of states and counties included Head Start: Home-Based (in 22 states and 329 counties), Home Instruction for Parents of Preschool Youngsters (in 17 states and 137 counties), and Healthy Start: Home Visiting (in 17 states and 176 counties).

In addition to reporting evidence-based home visiting models, most states reported some home visiting programs that were not implementing these models. In particular, 50 states reported programs that either did not specify a home visiting approach or reported implementing home visiting approaches that were not reported by any other states (see Appendix Table B.1 for a list). Some of these programs appeared to be using homegrown models, although some borrowed practices and curricula from nationally recognized home visiting models. Such programs were common; they were reported as operating in nearly 1,800 counties.

Identifying At-Risk Communities

Although home visiting services already existed in all states, MIECHV was created to fill a perceived gap in those services. In their needs assessments, states were asked to identify and provide data for at-risk communities, defined in the authorizing legislation as communities with concentrations of the following: premature birth, low birth weight, infant mortality, poverty, crime, domestic violence, high school dropouts, substance abuse, unemployment, or child maltreatment. In practice, most states identified counties or groups of counties as their at-risk communities and provided information at the county level.

The full set of indicators states reported for each of these communities is presented in Appendix C. It should be noted that most states provided information on most indicators, but states often could not provide all of the indicators exactly as they were requested. When states were unable to provide data on the requested indicator, they sometimes included information on a close substitute. For example, many states reported the nonmedical use of pain relievers in the past year rather than the nonmedical use of prescription drugs in the past month. In addition, while HRSA requested that states report the rate of "substantiated" child maltreatment, states responded using metrics such as the rate of "child abuse and neglect confirmations" and the "child victim rate." For this reason, rates for child maltreatment should not be compared across states. Appendix C contains the language of HRSA's request and the metric each state used in its assessment.

Table 2.2 summarizes information on four indicators — rates of premature birth, poverty, unemployment, and child maltreatment — that were selected to represent different categories of risk. For each indicator, the table compares the state average with the average for the communities chosen to receive MIECHV funds. In examining these indicators, it is important to remember that many states intended to support MIECHV-funded programs in the highest-need areas *within* the target communities. Thus, community averages may understate the level of risk in targeted areas.

Indicator values varied regionally.[26] A comparison of the indicators in Table 2.2 shows that states in the South (HRSA Regions 4 and 6) tended to have higher average indicator values than states in other parts of the country, and states in the Northeast (HRSA Regions 1-3) tended to have lower levels of poverty and unemployment.[27] Target community average values also tended to be higher in the South, indicating that states in the South identified target communities that were more disadvantaged than target communities in the rest of the country, which is not surprising given the higher values for these indicators in the southern states overall. While target communities in the Northeast were less disadvantaged than target communities in the South, states in the Northeast tended to have larger disparities between their target community averages and their state averages.

Table 2.3 summarizes the information presented in Table 2.2 by showing how many states had target communities with greater levels of disadvantage than their overall averages, and how much difference there was between the average target community and the state averages overall. As shown in Table 2.3, states generally selected communities that had relatively high rates of poverty: In 50 of the 53 states that provided this information, the average target community had a poverty rate that was higher than the state average. Often, the gap was considerable: In 34 states, the poverty rate in the average target community was greater than the state average rate by 25 percent or more.

Table 2.2. Selected Community Risk Indicators in Communities Chosen for MIECHV Funding, by State

Area	Premature Births[a](%)		Residents Livingin Poverty(%)		Residents Unemployed (%)		Child Maltreatment[b]	
	Target Community Average[c]	StateAverage	Target Community Average[c]	StateAverage	Target Community Average[c]	StateAverage	Target Community Average[c]	State Average
HRSA Region 1								
Connecticut[d]	11	11	24	12	8	6	28	1
Maine	9	9	14	13	10	9	13	13
Massachusetts	9	9	18	9	8	9	39	20
New Hampshire	10	10	11	8	6	6	545	315
Rhode Island	12	12	20	12	13	11	19	12
Vermont	11	9	11	9	8	7	6	5
HRSA Region 2								
New Jersey	11	10	17	6	7	4	-	-
New York	12	12	14	15	5	5	156	169
Puerto Rico	15	20	62	45	26	19	30	41
U.S. Virgin Islands	-	1	-	29	-	8	-	14
HRSA Region 3								
Delaware[d]	15	14	12	10	4	8	1	1
Maryland[d]	17	11	42	10	10	7	7	2
Pennsylvania	11	10	14	12	11	9	2	1
Virginia	12	11	19	10	6	4	5	3
West Virginia	15	12	22	17	9	10	-	14
District of Columbia	15	12	27	13	19	10	410	-
HRSA Region 4								
Alabama	-	17	27	16	16	10	8	9

Area	Premature Births[a](%)		Residents Livingin Poverty(%)		Residents Unemployed (%)		Child Maltreatment[b]	
	Target Community Average[c]	StateAverage	Target Community Average[c]	StateAverage	Target Community Average[c]	StateAverage	Target Community Average[c]	State Average
Florida[d]	14	14	25	22	6	7	51	40
Georgia	14	13	19	14	9	10	8	13
Kentucky	19	14	31	20	14	13	32	17
Mississippi	22	18	31	21	10	7	-	-
North Carolina	14	13	18	15	12	11	38	30
South Carolina	12	12	22	16	14	13	7	6
Tennessee	13	12	15	14	11	11	8	8
HRSA Region 5								
Illinois[e]	-	-	-	-	-	-	-	-
Indiana	12	11	24	17	22	19	-	11
Michigan	11	11	18	14	13	14	16	12
Minnesota	10	10	13	10	6	5	6	4
Ohio	14	13	17	13	11	10	11	9
Wisconsin	12	11	12	11	10	9	4	4
HRSA Region 6								
Arkansas	18	14	27	17	8	8	8	9
Louisiana[f]	15	14	23	18	10	7	-	-
New Mexico	12	11	25	17	11	8	27	16
Oklahoma	11	11	17	16	7	7	16	15
Texas	15	14	21	16	8	8	14	11
HRSA Region 7								
Iowa	10	9	16	11	8	7	33	18
Kansas	10	9	16	11	11	7	6	3
Missouri	17	13	24	14	7	6	6	5
Nebraska	8	10	14	10	4	3	10	7
HRSA Region 8								
Colorado	11	10	22	11	10	8	11	9
Montana[d]	8	8	22	19	7	7	51	38
North Dakot[a]	-	10	-	14	-	4	-	1
South Dakota	16	12	40	13	8	5	-	1
Utah	12	10	10	10	-	7	31	15
Wyoming	11	11	11	10	6	6	5	4

Table 2.2. (Continued)

Area	Premature Births[a] (%)		Residents Livingin Poverty (%)		Residents Unemployed (%)		Child Maltreatment[b]	
	Target Community Average[c]	StateAverage	Target Community Average[c]	StateAverage	Target Community Average[c]	StateAverage	Target Community Average[c]	State Average
HRSA Region 9								
Arizona	10	10	19	15	10	10	32	10
California	11	11	15	13	13	12	11	9
Hawaii	11	11	33	11	6	6	7	1
Nevada	11	11	12	11	14	14	13	10
American Samoa	-	-	61	61	30	30	-	-
Guam	3	5	60	20	25	-	-	2
Northern Mariana Islands	7	8	56	40	-	8	72	223
HRSA Region 10								
Alaska	11	11	7	9	7	8	67	61
Idaho	11	10	14	13	9	9	7	4
Oregon	11	10	17	14	11	11	18	13
Washington	12	11	15	11	12	9	73	44

Source: 2010 MIECHV state needs assessments.

Notes: In this table, "state" is used as shorthand for states, territories, and the District of Columbia.

HRSA = Health Resources and Services Administration.

Most states identified target communities as counties or groups of counties, so target community average data typically reflect county data; however, some states identified and reported data for smaller regions. Some states reported indicator data of a larger region to which a target community belonged when information was not available at the community level.

Unless otherwise noted, hyphens indicate instances when the state did not provide target community or state average data for the indicator.

[a] Defined as number of live births before 37 weeks of gestation/total number of live births.

[b] In their needs assessments, states reported indicators for child maltreatment that varied widely in both what they measured and how they were measured. Examples of child maltreatment indicators reported by states include substantiated child abuse cases, confirmed victims of child abuse and neglect, and overall child maltreatment. While most states reported the indicator by rates per 1,000, others reported percentages, total numbers, or other rates.

Because states reported this indicator so differently, values should not be compared between states. For more information on what HRSA requested and what states reported, see Appendix C.

[c] Some states did not report data on the indicators for all of their target communities. In those cases, the target community average only reflects the average of the target communities for which information was provided.

[d] This state reported a slight variation on the indicator for residents living in poverty. See the state's table in Appendix C for more information.

[e] Illinois reported data for its target communities as ranges of values and did not report data for the state, so averages were unavailable.

[f] For its child maltreatment indicator, Louisiana reported the percentage of child maltreatment cases that were substantiated. Since this measure was very different from the other measures states used for this indicator, it has been excluded from this table. See Appendix Table C.19 for more information.

Table 2.3. Number of States for Which Target Community Averages Are Less Than, Greater Than, or Much Greater Than State Averages, for Selected Community Risk Indicators

Target Community Average Is...	Premature Births[a]	Residents Living in Poverty	Residents Unemployed	Child Maltreatment[b]
Less than or equal to state average	10	3	13	7
Greater than state average	41	50	37	37
Greater by 0% - 25%	36	16	24	10
Greater by 25% or more	5	34	13	27
Total states with available information[c]	51	53	50	44

Source: 2010 MIECHV state needs assessments.

Notes: In this table, "state" is used as shorthand for states, territories, and the District of Columbia.

[a] Defined as number of live births before 37 weeks of gestation/total number of live births.

[b] In their needs assessments, states reported indicators for child maltreatment that varied widely in both what they measured and how they were measured. However, they typically did measure consistently for both their target communities and the state as a whole, allowing comparisons between the state and target community averages. For more information on what HRSA requested and what states reported, see Appendix C.

[c] Some states did not report data on these indicators for their target communities or did not include overall state averages. Some states also reported data in such a way that those data could not be included in this table.

For example, the Illinois needs assessment reported ranges of values for its indicators in each of its target communities, so it was not possible to calculate an average.

States also tended to select target communities with higher rates of premature birth, unemployment, and child maltreatment than their overall averages. In 27 of 44 states, the target community average rate of child maltreatment was higher than that of the state over-all by 25 percent or more; conversely, however, in seven states these average rates in target communities were actually lower than the state averages.

States' Proposed Plans for MIECHV Funding

Two types of MIECHV funding were made available from fiscal year (FY) 2010 through FY 2015: formula funding, which all states were eligible to receive, and competitive funding, which a limited number of states received following a competitive application process.

Table 2.4. Summary of Communities, Local Programs, Counties, and Models Proposed for FY 2010 and FY 2011 MIECHV Funding, Across States

	Average Value for States	Minimum Value for States	Maximum Value for States
Target communities proposed for funding	8	1	42
Local programs proposed for funding[a]			
Number	10	1	56
Percentage in metropolitan communities[b]	56	0	100
Percentage in nonmetropolitan communities[b]	43	0	100
Target counties proposed for funding			
Percentage of total counties targeted	30	2	100
Percentage with home visiting services reported prior to MIECHV[c]	96	50	100

	Average Value for States	Minimum Value for States	Maximum Value for States
Evidence-based models proposed for funding	2	1	4

Sources: FY 2010 and FY 2011 state plans, the first round of competitive grant applications, and 2010 MIEHCV state needs assessments.

Notes: In this table, "state" is used as shorthand for states, territories, and the District of Columbia. North Dakota is excluded from this table because it did not submit state plans for MIECHV funding. The information in this table is limited to what was proposed in the FY 2010 and FY 2011 state plans and the first round of competitive grant applications. State plans for MIECHV funding continued to evolve after these documents were submitted. Target communities are the communities that states selected to receive MIECHV funding. They can cover areas in one or more target counties. Proposed local programs are the programs that have been selected to implement evidence-based home visiting programs with MIECHV funding. In some cases, a target community will have more than one local program.

[a] Local organizations are counted once for each model they are funded to operate; for example, if a local organization is funded to operate two models, it is counted as two local programs.

[b] To designate counties as metropolitan or nonmetropolitan, this report follows the Department of Agriculture Economic Research Service's Rural-Urban Continuum Codes classification scheme. See Economic Research Service (2013a). American Samoa, Guam, the Northern Mariana Islands, and the U.S. Virgin Islands were not designated under this scheme. The local programs in those territories were assumed to be nonmetropolitan, based on definitions from the Office of Management and Budget. See Economic Research Service (2013b).

[c] Montana did not provide information on which counties were served by pre-MIECHV home visiting programs. Therefore Montana was excluded from this row.

For each fiscal year, states developed and submitted plans for how they intended to use the funds, and these plans were expected to draw upon information from their needs assessments. This report summarizes the earliest plans that were submitted, which are the FY 2010 and 2011 formula funding applications and FY 2011 competitive grant applications for states that received competitive grants. Although states continued to have opportunities to revise their plans for MIECHV funds with each round of funding, these earliest versions provide valuable insight into how state plans were related to their needs assessments, which had been completed shortly before. They are summarized in Table 2.4. More detailed information on states' plans is presented in Appendix D. It should be noted that neither Table 2.4 nor

Appendix D reflects any changes in plans states have made in more recent years.

Table 2.4 shows that the average state proposed using MIECHV funds in eight communities, although some states proposed funds for only one community while one state proposed funding for 42. Communities often included more than one local program, and the average state proposed using MIECHV funds to support 10 local programs. In the average state, about 56 percent of the local programs for which states proposed to use MIECHV funding were metropolitan.[28]

The average state proposed to use MIECHV funds in 30 percent of its counties. Although the target communities were the ones states had previously identified as being most in need of home visiting, states also reported that 96 percent of the counties corresponding to these target communities did have home visiting services prior to MIECHV. This suggests that existing programs in the neediest communities were not meeting all of those areas' needs.

As noted earlier, the legislation that created MIECHV required states to spend a majority of those funds on evidence-based home visiting models. Table 2.5, which summarizes the models identified by states for MIECHV support, confirms that most states planned to use all of their MIECHV funds to support evidence-based models. In their early plans only eight states reported that they planned to use MIECHV funds for promising, non-evidence-based approaches. Most states (33) planned to expand the use of evidence-based home visiting models that were already in operation, but eight states proposed supporting evidence-based models that were not already operating within their borders, and 14 states proposed to do both.

Table 2.5. Summary of FY 2010 and FY 2011 State Plans for MIECHV Funding

States	Counties[a]	
Proposed use of funds		
Expand existing evidence-based models only	33	158
Fund new evidence-based models only	8	176
Expand existing evidence-based models and fund new evidence-based models	14	53
Fund promising approaches[b]	8	-
Evidence-based model use[c]		
Early Head Start - Home Based Program Option	17	49
Family Check-Up	0	0

States	Counties[a]	
Healthy Families America	39	177
Healthy Steps	2	6
Home Instruction for Parents of Preschool Youngsters	7	30
Nurse-Family Partnership	40	169
Parents as Teachers	29	123

Sources: FY 2010 and FY 2011 state plans, the first round of competitive grant applications, and 2010 MIECHV state needs assessments.

Notes: In this table, "state" is used as shorthand for states, territories, and the District of Columbia. North Dakota is excluded from this table because the state did not submit plans for MIECHV funding.

The information in this table is limited to what was proposed in the FY 2010 and FY 2011 state plans and the first round of competitive grant applications. State plans for MIECHV funding continued to evolve after these documents were submitted.

[a] While some states identified target communities that were not counties, this table summarizes information at the county level to be consistent across states. One state and some additional target communities in other states were not included in the county-level analyses in this table because information was not provided on either which models were operating before MIECHV or which models were proposed to be implemented for all of the target communities.

[b] States were allowed to commit up to 25 percent of their funding to support promising approaches that did not qualify as evidence-based models at the time they were creating their state plans. In this table, a state was counted as planning to use a promising approach if it mentioned an intention to use a promising approach in its FY 2011 state plan or first-round competitive grant application, even if it had not yet decided on a particular model to use. Information on the number of counties in which states proposed to operate promising approaches is unavailable because many states had not yet reached that stage of planning.

[c] This table only includes information for the first seven models that were designated as evidence-based. Additional models have since been designated as evidence-based, but they were not able to be included in the FY 2010 and FY 2011 state plans.

Although the HomVEE review had found seven evidence-based home visiting models by the time the first state plans were developed, Table 2.5 indicates that states planned to use MIECHV primarily for only four of them: Nurse-Family Partnership (40 states), Healthy Families America (39 states), Parents as Teachers (29 states), and Early Head Start (17 states). On average, states proposed funding two evidence-based models, and 10 states planned to fund four evidence-based models (not shown in Table 2.5). Among the three other evidence-based models from which states were able to select, seven states proposed to fund Home Instruction for Parents of Preschool Youngsters, two states pro-posed to fund Healthy Steps, and no states proposed to fund Family Check-Up.

Findings from Interviews with 12 MIECHV State Administrators

To provide context for the states' needs assessments and planning processes, this section summarizes interviews with MIECHV state administrators from the 12 states that are participating in MIHOPE (see Section 3 for a description of how those 12 states were selected). These interviews provide insights into how state-level agencies and leaders responded to MIECHV and planned for its implementation, including the types of factors that were considered outside the documents that states submitted. The information summarized below centers on the following questions:

- How did states compile and use the needs assessments to make decisions about allocating funds and expanding home visiting services in local communities?
- What factors did the 12 states consider when using the needs assessments to select communities for MIECHV funding?
- What factors did they consider in identifying and selecting evidence-based models?
- How did states use the needs assessments to target priority populations?

Developing the State Needs Assessments

Several state administrators noted that it was difficult to complete needs assessments in the time allowed by HRSA. Nonetheless, all 12 states were able to form cross-agency collaborations, as encouraged by HRSA, to support the development and integration of a broad network of early childhood systems and programs. These collaborations were formed most often among departments of public health, human services, and education.

Many states also included nonprofit and educational organizations with investments in early child development or maternal and child health in these collaborative groups, and some included representatives from national evidence-based models that were already operating in the state. A few states noted particular underserved or vulnerable communities that were of concern to the leaders of their collaborative groups, including Native American or refugee populations. In those few states, the agency that had been designated to receive the state's MIECHV funds added representatives from tribal affairs offices or migrant and refugee services to the group completing the needs assessment.

These collaborations were formed largely to discuss how to gather, pool, and analyze data for the states' needs assessments. States had slightly different processes for selecting and deciding on the data and constructs to use to measure risk indicators for their needs assessments. Two state administrators noted that they considered whether recent data were available, underscoring their concern that numbers from five years earlier, for example, might be misleading given recent demographic shifts in some areas (caused by, for example, new immigrant populations) and the effects of the recession that began in 2007. One of these administrators further recounted that for metropolitan areas the data were recent and relatively easy to assemble but that for other areas the data were older.

After collecting information on the indicators required by HRSA, one state identified where counties ranked across indicators. That state also developed a survey of county-level health directors to inquire about other possible factors or measures. The results of this first round of data were used to develop the initial needs assessment. A request for information put out by HRSA following states' initial needs assessments provided an opportunity for this state to gather information below the county level.[29]

Another state administrator noted that some of the information requested as part of the needs assessments (in particular, information related to the prevalence of substance abuse) was not available at the local level. In this case, the state did not include any information at the local or state level for this indicator.

Making Decisions about Targeting Communities

All state administrators said they could not fund services in all of their high-risk communities. They therefore had to be thoughtful about how they could allocate funds. Most states used the indicators summarized earlier in this section to identify the counties or groups of counties that had the greatest needs. The state plans and needs assessments were always used in identifying these communities, as most of the administrators conveyed a desire to make transparent decisions based on evidence. The majority of states used the needs assessments to create overall risk scores, typically cumulative summaries of all the indicators that were considered, and targeted those communities that scored the worst.

In determining risk scores, several states used both quantitative indicators and qualitative information. At least two of the 12 states, for example, interviewed local stakeholders to learn about nuances not captured by the needs-assessment indicators. One state conducted focus groups with community residents to understand their concerns about maternal, infant, and child health and well-being. The state used this information to understand the different types of need present in the community, although this information was essentially supplemental to the quantitative risk-scoring process.

Although all states used an evidence-driven process, several administrators from states with very large metropolitan areas noted that discussions about how to identify and define geographic areas of risk were at times contentious. One state administrator noted, "There is a lot of political strain going on based on [geographic] areas of focus." That debate, however, was not about differing poverty levels per se, but rather was driven by variations in density: The poor are more sparsely distributed in the state's less urban areas than in its major city and the adjacent communities. Indeed, a few states strove to direct MIECHV funding to both urban and rural areas. In other states, however, other considerations made it difficult to achieve such even representation. As one state administrator revealed, "Some counties are fairly high-risk but they have no infrastructure or individuals in some areas to run a program." Another similarly noted that some counties whose indicators showed that they had high levels of risk were not chosen for funding because they did not appear to have strong infrastructure. Thus, states had to balance two goals — reaching the highest-risk communities and ensuring that home visiting programs could be adequately implemented— and varied in how they did so.

For states that received both formula and competitive funding, the competitive funds allowed them to serve additional high-risk communities. As one administrator noted, "When the competitive funds came, we just continued down the list." A few states also chose to further expand programs in areas that had received formula funding. One state used MIECHV competitive funds to focus more acutely on a particular health concern (infant mortality) and to target communities that had the highest racial disparities in that area.

Selecting Evidence-Based Models

As recounted by many of the 12 state administrators, using the HomVEE review as an aid to model selection illustrated a shift toward "evidence-based" decisions in the field of home visiting. Several administrators noted that MIECHV did not lead their states to expand local, "homegrown" home visiting programs, but moved them toward the broader use of models that had demonstrated rigorous evidence of affecting specific domains.

All states looked for evidence-based models that matched the needs of their populations. States weighed several considerations in choosing which models to implement. Many state administrators used the HomVEE findings to determine which models were likely to meet the needs of targeted communities. One state, in fact, brought in Nurse-Family Partnership, which previously did not have a presence there, based on evidence that the model improved maternal and infant health (including birth outcomes), areas of particular concern for that state. Two states noted they emphasized serving teenage and young mothers, which supported their decisions to fund Nurse-Family Partnership programs in addition to other evidence-based programs. The timing of client enrollment proved important as well because several states were particularly focused on improving prenatal maternal health and infant health at birth. This focus led them to make a higher priority of Nurse-Family Partnership or Healthy Families America programs, which have both shown positive effects on birth outcomes. Conversely, another state noted that Nurse-Family Partnership could be "limiting" because it only enrolls first-time mothers. This state allocated MIECHV funding to Nurse-Family Partnership programs, but also chose to fund other programs that enroll women who are not first-time mothers.

As discussed in Section 3, all of the states participating in MIHOPE implemented two or more of the evidence-based models. According to the MIECHV administrator interviews with the 12 MIHOPE states, as of 2013 only one state had made any change to the original models selected in its FY 2011 plan, adding a model to its original list. As described earlier, FY 2010 and 2011 data show that as of then only eight states had funded more than three models. One state administrator explained that because of concerns regarding gathering comparable data across the different models (which use different data-collection and monitoring systems), working with more than two or three models seemed like it would make timely data collection and reporting too burdensome.

States usually funded national models that were operating within their borders prior to MIECHV. In order to "hit the ground running," state administrators often thought it was best to either fund agencies that were already functioning or expand existing models to new communities or agencies. A few states allowed local communities or programs to decide which evidence-based models to implement based on the populations they were serving.

Identifying Target Populations

State administrators reported that MIECHV funds would target populations with at least one risk-related characteristic of compromised health and well-being, including populations explicitly identified in the authorizing legislation such as low-income families, teenage mothers, and families with mental health and substance-use concerns. A few state administrators also mentioned their attempts to target areas with military families, which are also a priority population. However, one administrator noted that this proved challenging because military families in the state tended to be located in training bases and to be transient, residing in one location for only a few months at a time. This made it difficult to provide services designed to last months or years in a stable manner.

Perhaps because the populations and communities highlighted by the authorizing legislation are broad and at times overlapping, a few states identified their own concerns and priorities as they interpreted the definition of high-risk populations. One state administrator, for example, noted that concerns about racial and ethnic disparities prompted the state to collect information during the needs assessment process on the racial and ethnic composition of communities. Another state wanted local programs to focus on transient and homeless populations, in addition to populations with other risk factors. A different state was particularly concerned about children born with inheritable diseases and conditions. This was admittedly a very small number of families, but those families were to be approached by local programs and given a high priority for services if they desired them.

For the most part, however, state administrators typically conveyed that choosing high-risk communities and working with evidence-based models that target disadvantaged families would result in outreach to and enrollment of high-risk families. As one state administrator recounted, "Model selection was based on the risk factors present in that community and the model's ability to or what research said they could best handle as risk factors. And then we let the models say what they target. We didn't say to them, 'Go beyond this.'" States appeared to be cautious about not appearing overly officious in managing local programs' enrollment processes, and to recognize that community-based agencies understood the needs of the families in their areas the best.

Nevertheless, a few states asked local programs (including those implementing Early Head Start, Healthy Families America, and Parents as Teachers) to focus more heavily on enrolling women during pregnancy than they had in the past. Conversely, at least one state told local programs that they should not enroll pregnant women because their national model had not exhibited evidence of improving pregnancy-related outcomes, according to the HomVEE review.

Conclusion

States were able to identify at-risk communities in need of home visiting services, and MIECHV encouraged states to spend resources developing and newly implementing evidence-based home visiting models, especially the four models being studied in MIHOPE. The next section describes how the MIHOPE team used state plans to decide which states might be the most appropriate for the study, and how that led to a process that resulted in 12 states being asked to participate.

Section 3. Selection of MIHOPE States and Local Programs

As reported in Section 2, funds for the Maternal, Infant, and Early Childhood Home Visiting Program (MIECHV) were used throughout the country primarily to support local home visiting programs running one of four national evidence-based models. Because those models were chosen by at least 10 states, they are being studied in the Mother, Infant, and Home Visiting Program Evaluation (MIHOPE). Although states and local programs were required to participate in MIHOPE if asked, the study did not have enough resources to include a nationally representative set of local home visiting programs, but planned to choose a set of local programs that were representative of the diversity of MIECHV sites. It therefore sought to include a total of about 85 local programs from 12 states, which would provide enough local programs to allow the study to explore variation in services and impacts across different locations but few enough states to make the costs of enrolling families and collecting data manageable. This section describes the process of selecting states and local programs for the study and summarizes selected characteristics of the local programs and their staff.

Main Findings

- **As of May 2014, 12 states and 88 local home visiting programs were participating in MIHOPE.** States were chosen to represent all regions of the country. Local programs were chosen to provide a roughly equal number of programs operating each national evidence-based home visiting model, to provide as many programs operating in nonmetropolitan areas as feasible, and to provide enough families overall to provide reliable estimates of the effects of home visiting on outcomes for families and children.
- **Most local programs operate in large urban areas.** Over three-quarters of local programs included in MIHOPE operate in metropolitan counties. This is greater than the percentage of MIECHV-funded programs in metropolitan counties nationally as reported in the state plans (56 percent, as discussed in Section 2). This is because many rural programs considered for MIHOPE were not large enough to contribute at least 40 families to the study while still allowing for the ethical creation of a control group.
- **The study includes fewer local programs operating Early Head Start-Home Based Program Option than the other evidence-based models.** As noted in Section 2, of the four evidence-based models being studied in MIHOPE, initial MIECHV funds were used least frequently to support the expansion of Early Head Start programs. As a result, only 19 of the study's 88 programs are operating Early Head Start, compared with 26 local programs for Healthy Families America, 22 for Nurse-Family Partnership, and 21 for Parents as Teachers.

Selecting States

Initial Identification of High-Priority States

As one of its first activities, the study team reviewed the 2010 and 2011 state plans for MIECHV funds in order to determine which states were most likely to contribute the right mix and number of local programs to the study.

This resulted in 31 states being considered a high priority for study participation because they met the following criteria:

- **They were planning to implement more than one of the four evidence-based models being studied by MIHOPE.** This would help analyses distinguish between the influence of a particular state and the influence of a particular national model.
- **They were planning to support five or more eligible local programs.** Such states were considered a higher priority because they would help the study achieve its goal of choosing about 85 local programs from 12 states.
- **They mentioned an intention to serve military families.** Since the legislation that created MIECHV includes military families in its list of target populations, the study sought to include states whose local programs served such families.

Final Selection of States

Since the study did not have the resources to conduct research in all 31 high-priority states, the study team chose a subset for further outreach based on the following criteria:

- **They would represent each of four geographic regions of the United States** using combinations of regions defined by the Administration for Children and Families and the Health Resources and Services Administration. These corresponded to the Northeast,[30] South,[31] Midwest and Plains,[32] and Mountain and West.[33]
- **They would allow the study to include a similar number of local programs for each of the four evidence-based national models.**
- **They would allow the study to include some local programs operating in nonmetropolitan areas.**

Based on these criteria, the study team began discussions with 10 states early in 2012. The team made contact with each state to assess its progress in implementing MIECHV, including whether other research on home visiting was taking place in the state and the status of decisions regarding MIECHV funding. After these discussions, the study team began discussions with seven additional high-priority states to ensure more equal model distribution and geographic diversity.

These discussions also revealed that the targeted states could not provide as many Early Head Start programs as programs for the other three national evidence-based models. This was consistent with the state plans (discussed in Section 2), which showed that fewer states chose to use MIECHV funds for Early Head Start than for the other three models. An examination of other high-priority states identified a cluster of newly eligible Early Head Start programs in several states, which were added to the list of actively recruited states.

The following 12 states are participating in MIHOPE: California, Georgia, Illinois, Iowa, Kansas, Michigan, Nevada, New Jersey, Pennsylvania, South Carolina, Washington, and Wisconsin. In Figure 3.1, these states are highlighted in gray.

Selecting Local Programs

MIHOPE's initial goal was to select approximately 85 local programs across the four national evidence-based models. Although Section 2 indicated that states planned to use MIECHV funds to support several hundred such local home visiting programs, local programs had to meet several criteria to be included in MIHOPE.

- They had to have been in operation for at least two years when they entered the study.
- They had to be able to recruit enough families to fill program slots and to allow for a randomly chosen control group.
- They had to be located where control group members would be unlikely to have access to alternative evidence-based home visiting services.
- They had to have more than one MIECHV-funded home visitor so that evaluation activities would be spread across program staff members.
- They had to contribute to the goal of roughly equal representation of the four evidence-based national models.
- They could not be operating in "frontier locations," which included both counties with fewer than 2,500 people and urban areas with fewer than 20,000 people that were not adjacent to a metropolitan area. These areas were excluded to reduce the costs of recruiting families and collecting information.

In states with more eligible programs than were needed for the study, the study team randomly chose programs to participate, with some weighting toward programs in rural counties where possible.

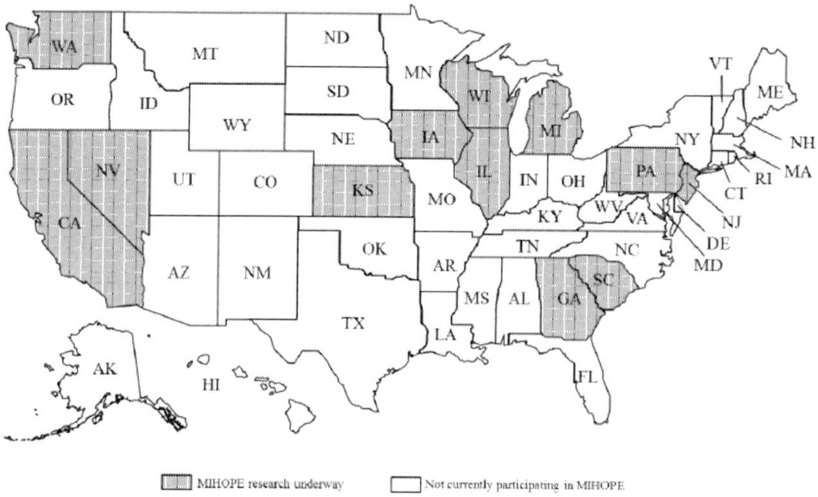

Figure 3.1. Map of MIHOPE States.

To identify and choose local programs for the study, study team members visited most local programs that were receiving MIECHV funds and had been in operation for at least two years. The team presented an overview of MIHOPE and facilitated a discussion about the feasibility of participation in the study given the programs' administrative structures, implementation schedules, and sizes. Follow-up phone calls with local programs being considered for MIHOPE were used to learn more about issues such as whether a program received enough referrals to provide at least 40 families to the study while still providing a control group. In a few cases, local programs were not considered because the national model developer expressed concerns about how services were being implemented there.

This process resulted in the selection of 87 local programs, which entered MIHOPE between October 2012 and February 2014. An eighty-eighth local program was added in December 2014. Table 3.1 shows the breakdown of local programs by state and geographical region, and by national model. As Figure 3.1 and Table 3.1 illustrate, there are MIHOPE states in the Northeast, Midwest, South, and Mountain and West, although there are more states in the Midwest than elsewhere. As described earlier, MIECHV funding is in part based on a formula, which resulted in more populous states receiving more funding. Therefore, there was considerable variation in the number of local programs that received MIECHV funding in each state. This is true for the number of local programs selected for MIHOPE in each state as well; it ranges from 3 (Nevada and South Carolina) to 14 (Illinois). The average number of local programs per state is 7⅓.

Although the study sought to include a similar number of local programs for each of the four national models, there are more Healthy Families America programs than the other three models, and there are fewer Early Head Start programs than the other models, which reflects the number of eligible local programs operating each national model in the selected states.

By design, each state has local programs representing at least two national models. Slightly more than half of the participating states have local programs representing three or more national models. This may in part be due to the expansion of more home visiting programs with competitive funding; MIHOPE states all received competitive MIECHV funds in addition to formula-based funds.

Characteristics of Local Programs and Home Visitors

Table 3.2 shows some characteristics of local programs when they entered the study, including the type of agency implementing each program, the years the program had been in operation, its enrollment capacity, the type of county it served, and the proportion of its funding that came from MIECHV. Some of these characteristics could be associated with how programs are implemented at the local level, and, in turn, how they affect families. For example, studies of human-service programs have produced some evidence that program effects are associated with factors such as program maturity.[34] Also, the type of implementing agency can shape the types of resources local programs have access to and the degree to which they focus on linking families to particular types of services.

Information on local program characteristics was provided by program managers around the time programs started participating in MIHOPE. The majority of local programs (60 percent) are run by community-based nonprofit agencies; others are implemented by local health departments, school districts, health care organizations, or other types of organizations.

Table 3.1. MIHOPE States and Programs

State	Region	Total Programs	EHS	HFA	NFP	PAT
California	Mountain and West	6	0	1	5	0
Georgia	South	6	1	3	0	2
Illinois	Midwest and Plains	14	1	5	1	7
Iowa	Midwest and Plains	11	4	7	0	0
Kansas	Midwest and Plains	8	2	2	0	4
Michigan	Midwest and Plains	7	3	2	2	0
Nevada	Mountain and West	3	2	0	1	0
New Jersey	Northeast	12	0	4	5	3
Pennsylvania	Northeast	8	4	0	2	2
South Carolina	South	3	0	1	2	0
Washington	Mountain and West	6	0	0	4	2
Wisconsin	Midwest and Plains	4	2	1	0	1
Sample size		88	19	26	22	21

Source: MIHOPE site-selection team.

Note: EHS = Early Head Start -Home Based Program Option, HFA = Healthy Families America, NFP = Nurse-Family Partnership, PAT = Parents as Teachers.

Over three-quarters of local programs serve families in metropolitan counties. Although the design of MIHOPE called for the study to select programs to represent both urban and rural counties, it proved to be difficult to include states that both funded multiple home visiting models and funded programs in rural counties. As a result, MIHOPE included many of the most populous states in the country, which limited the number of counties that were deemed to be rural. Lastly, even within the populous MIHOPE states, there were some local programs in rural counties that were excluded due to other factors. For example, in one state, five programs in rural counties were deemed to be poor candidates for MIHOPE due to the small sizes of their communities, the proximity of other home visiting programs, or a demand for services insufficient to provide a control group for the study.

The vast majority of local programs had been operating for six or more years when they began participating in the study. This reflects both the fact that states used MIECHV funds primarily to expand existing programs (as described in Section 2) and MIHOPE's selection of local programs that had been in operation for at least two years. As might be expected given that most of them existed for some time prior to MIECHV, programs reported considerable funding from other sources. In fact, MIECHV provides less than

20 percent of the funding of nearly half of the local programs participating in MIHOPE. For about 12 percent of local programs, however, MIECHV provides 75 percent or more of the program's financial resources.

Table 3.2. Basic Characteristics of Local Programs at Entry into Study

Characteristic (%)	Local Programs
Type of local implementing agency	
Community-based nonprofit	60
Local health department	18
School district	10
Health care organization	5
Other [a]	8
County served[b]	
Metropolitan	78
Nonmetropolitan	14
Both	9
Years program had been in operation[c]	
2 to 3	1
4 to 5	12
6 or more	87
Enrollment capacity[d]	
≤ 50 families	11
51-100 families	28
> 100 families	61
Proportion of funding from MIECHV	
Less than 20%	46
20% -49%	29
50% -74%	13
75% or more	12
Sample size	80

Sources: Calculations based on data from the MIHOPE program manager baseline survey and the MIHOPE site-selection team.

Notes: Rounding may cause slight discrepancies in sums.

[a] Other types of organizations include: state-funded institution of higher education, local government and cooperative extension university, and social-service nonprofit.

[b] To designate counties as metropolitan or nonmetropolitan, this report follows the Department of Agriculture Economic Research Service's Rural-Urban Continuum Codes classification scheme. See Economic Research Service (2013a).

[c] Years using the specific national model in use at study entry.

[d] The number of families served at any one time.

The majority of local programs reported enrollment capacity of more than 100 families, which is considered relatively large for a local home visiting program. This may also reflect the fact that the study was limited to programs that had more than one home visitor and that could contribute at least 40 families to the study.

Table 3.3 shows some variation in staff characteristics such as age, race and ethnicity, educational background, and prior experience providing home visiting services. Some of these characteristics, such as educational background and experience in home visiting, may indicate differences in skills in working with families, which in turn might be associated with how effectively staff members deliver services. Other attributes of home visitors, such as their psychological well-being, can also influence the services they deliver.[35]

About a quarter of home visitors employed at local programs were less than 30 years old and slightly more than half were less than 40 years old. This is consistent with other studies suggesting that most home visitors are less than 40 years old.[36] Supervisors tended to be older: 40 percent were more than 50 years old. Home visitors and supervisors were also more likely to identify themselves as non-Hispanic white than any other race or ethnicity.

About three-quarters of home visitors and nearly all supervisors had at least a bachelor's degree. It is notable that such a high proportion of home visitors had bachelors' degrees since Nurse-Family Partnership is the only one of the four national models to require this level of education for home visitors. This is consistent with a recent cross-model study of evidence-based home visiting that found that 79 percent of home visitors had a bachelor's degree or higher; earlier studies have reported rates of bachelor's degrees among home visitors ranging from 32 percent to 72 percent.[37]

In general, the national models have qualifications for home visitor employment that are focused on personal characteristics and experience working with families. In MIHOPE, half the home visitors had no experience providing home visiting services prior to their current positions but a quarter had more than five years of prior experience. This pattern holds true for supervisors as well.

Conclusion

MIHOPE used a systematic approach to determine which of the dozens of states and hundreds of local home visiting programs were the best candidates for meeting the study's goals of recruiting the desired number of families across about 85 local home visiting programs in 12 states. The process resulted in a selection of states that represented every region of the country and local programs that provided substantial representation for each of the four evidence-based home visiting models being studied. The next section describes the characteristics of families recruited into the study through January 15, 2014.

Table 3.3. Characteristics of Home Visitors and Supervisors

Characteristic (%)	Home Visitors	Supervisors
Age		
29 or under	27	8
30-39	29	32
40-49	24	20
50 or older	20	40
Race/ethnicity		
Hispanic	20	8
Non-Hispanic, white	57	74
Non-Hispanic, black	16	12
Asian	2	3
Other/multiracial	5	4
Educational and employment background		
Highest level of education		
High school/General Educational Development (GED) certificate or less	3	0
Vocational/technical training or some college	11	3
Associate's degree or training program degree	12	0
Bachelor's degree	60	62
Master's degree or higher	15	36
Prior experience providing home visiting services		
None	50	38
Less than 1 year	6	3
1-2 years	10	7
3-5 years	10	20
More than 5 years	24	33
Sample size	440	117

Sources: Calculations based on data from the MIHOPE baseline home visitor survey and the MIHOPE baseline supervisor survey.

Note: Percentages may not sum to 100 because of rounding.

SECTION 4. CHARACTERISTICS OF FAMILIES ENROLLED IN MIHOPE

This section provides the first glimpse of the women who have enrolled in the Mother and Infant Home Visiting Program Evaluation (MIHOPE) using information from surveys conducted with the women when they entered the study and observations of their home environments at that time. As noted in earlier sections, women were eligible for MIHOPE if they were pregnant or had children under 6 months old. Information on participating families provides some insights into the challenges faced by women who receive home visiting, which should be reflected in the types of services that the programs aim to provide. The information can also shed light on which subgroups are likely to be large enough to analyze in later MIHOPE reports, filling a gap in the literature noted by the Home Visiting Evidence of Effectiveness (HomVEE) review (as discussed in Section 1). Finally, it provides information on the extent to which states successfully targeted the types of families identified in their plans and emphasized as a high priority by the Patient Protection and Affordable Care Act.[38]

Because recruitment into the study continues, this section reports characteristics of families who entered the study by January 15, 2014. This includes 1,652 families, or slightly more than a third of the families who will eventually enroll in the study. The overall characteristics of study families may change when enrollment has been completed, but such changes are expected to be small.

Main Findings

- **Enrollees face a number of risks for poor outcomes for them and their children.** They were fairly young when they joined the study, with 37 percent of the sample between the ages of 15 and 20. The vast majority of women did not have schooling beyond high school. Over a third had smoked within the previous two years and a third reported using illegal drugs or binge drinking before becoming pregnant. Finally, about a third reported depressive symptoms.
- **MIECHV programs participating in MIHOPE have targeted most of the high-priority populations mentioned in the Affordable Care Act.** These include pregnant women under age 21, families who

have a history of substance abuse or who are in need of substance-abuse treatment, and families with tobacco users in the home.

- **There are few differences among the four evidence-based home visiting models in the families they have enrolled.** Levels of intimate partner violence, substance abuse, mental health concerns, and maternal education are similar in the families served by each of the four national models. The main differences in families across models is that Nurse-Family Partnership programs enrolled younger women than programs running the other evidence-based models, and all women who enrolled in Nurse-Family Partnership were pregnant (because of the model's eligibility requirements) compared with about half of the women enrolled in the other three national models.

Table 4.1. Selected Maternal and Household Characteristics, by Pregnancy Status at Enrollment

Characteristic	Total	Women Who Enrolled During Pregnancy	Women Who Enrolled After Giving Birth
Maternal			
Average age (years)	23.4	22.7	24.9***
Age 15-20 (%)	36.9	43.3	23.5***
Pregnancy status (%)			
Pregnant			
Less than 28 weeks	51.6	76.2	NA
More than 28 weeks	16.1	23.8	NA
Given birth	32.3	NA	100.0
Pregnant when enrolled and under 21 years old (%)	29.3	43.3	NA
Race/ethnicity (%)			
Hispanic	33.6	36.3	27.7***
Non-Hispanic, white	25.3	22.2	31.9***
Non-Hispanic, black	31.0	30.6	31.9
Asian	1.5	1.3	1.7
Other/multiracial	8.6	9.5	6.6*
Language other than English spoken in the home (%)	34.6	36.5	30.5**

Characteristic	Total	Women Who Enrolled During Pregnancy	Women Who Enrolled After Giving Birth
Ability to speak English self-rated as "not very well" or "not at all" (%)	7.9	6.7	10.3**
Household and family (%)			
Child's father lives in the home[a]	42.4	39.0	49.6***
Other adult relative lives in the home[b]	49.7	56.5	35.6***
A nonadult sibling of the child lives in the home[c]	34.2	25.7	51.9***
Moved more than once in the past year	22.0	24.0	17.8***
Family member is serving in the military[d]	1.0	0.7	1.6
Sample size	1,652	1,119	533

Source: Calculations based on data from the MIHOPE family baseline survey.

Notes: NA = not applicable.

A chisquared test was applied to differences between the characteristics of women who enrolled prenatally and women who enrolled postnatally, for categorical variables. A t-test was applied to differences in age between the women who enrolled prenatally and women who enrolled postnatally. Statistical significance levels are indicated as follows: *** = 1 percent, ** = 5 percent, * = 10 percent.

[a] Includes the child's biological father as well as the child's adoptive father or stepfather.

[b] Includes any relative who is age 18 or older, other than the child's biological mother, biological father, adoptive father, or stepfather.

[c] Includes stepsiblings.

[d] Includes the child's mother and her partner or spouse.

Social and Demographic Characteristics

Table 4.1 shows some of the social and demographic characteristics of MIHOPE families when they entered the study. Some groups, such as military families and pregnant women under 21 years of age, are shown because the authorizing legislation identified them as priorities. Other characteristics shown are relevant to understanding the risk profiles of families served by local programs in MIHOPE, including maternal age, maternal race and ethnicity, pregnancy status, maternal linguistic acculturation, household composition, and housing mobility. Since women who enroll in home visiting when they are pregnant face different challenges and have different needs than those who enroll after giving birth, Table 4.1 compares characteristics of pregnant women with those of postpartum women (as do several other tables in this section).

As shown in Table 4.1, women in the MIHOPE sample were young at the time they enrolled, with an average age of 23 (slightly younger for pregnant women). Almost 40 percent of the women were between 15 and 20 years old. Being younger (particularly being younger than 20) is associated with greater risk of poor birth outcomes and delays in child development,[39] although these relationships may be driven by differences in socioeconomic factors such as income, marital status, and education.[40]

As expected (since women eligible for MIHOPE had to be pregnant or have recently given birth) the majority of women were pregnant at the time they enrolled in the study, and over 40 percent who enrolled prenatally were under the age of 21. More than half the women enrolled when less than 28 weeks pregnant — one of the Nurse-Family Partnership eligibility criteria — which in part reflects the fact that 28 percent of the sample was enrolled through Nurse-Family Partnership programs (with 13 percent coming from Early Head Start-Home Based Program Option programs, 32 percent from Healthy Families America, and 28 percent from Parents as Teachers).

The sample is racially and ethnically diverse, and almost evenly distributed across the three largest racial/ethnic groups in the country: 34 percent are Hispanic, 25 percent are non-Hispanic white, and 31 percent are non-Hispanic black. Those who enrolled after giving birth are significantly more likely to be non-Hispanic white. Corresponding to the number that are Hispanic, about a third of the sample spoke a language other than English in the home. Only 8 percent of women reported poor English-speaking ability. Although a small subgroup, enrollees who do not speak English may be more challenging to serve if home visitors or other community service providers do not speak the mother's native language. Research has also shown that the acculturative process among first-generation immigrants—which often includes the loss of one's native language and the adoption of negative health behaviors and movement away from ethnic support networks — creates risk for chronic health conditions and mental health problems.[41]

Overall, it was uncommon for MIHOPE enrollees to live alone. Half of the women reported living with other relatives, perhaps reflecting how young many of them were. Among the participants who were living with relatives, about 42 percent were living with their parents or parents-in-law (not shown). Women who enrolled in home visiting after giving birth were more likely to be living with the child's biological father, adoptive father, or stepfather (50 percent) than women who enrolled during pregnancy (39 percent). Still, half of the women who enrolled after birth were living apart from the child's father or father figure.

About 22 percent of the sample reported moving more than once in the past year. Frequent moves can be a proxy for transience and unstable housing, particularly if there appears to be a consistent pattern of moves over several consecutive years. The prevalence of recent moves among the MIHOPE sample is slightly lower than the rate found in a study of housing mobility across 10 U.S. cities, in which about one in four low-income families had moved in the previous year.[42]

Only a handful (about 1 percent) of women enrolled in MIHOPE had a family member in the military, suggesting that MIHOPE programs and their communities might not have high concentrations of military families or be located near military bases. Again, this sample is not necessarily representative of the communities home visiting programs serve, given the site-selection criteria described in Section 3.

Characteristics Related to Outcome Domains

The remainder of the section describes baseline characteristics of MIHOPE families related to five outcome domains identified by the authorizing legislation: (1) prenatal, maternal, and newborn health; (2) child health and development; (3) parenting skills; (4) crime and domestic violence; and (5) family economic self-sufficiency. [43] The legislation also identified two other outcome domains — school readiness and academic achievement, and referrals and coordination — that are not discussed here because they could not be assessed when families entered the study. Specifically, school readiness and academic achievement could not be assessed because children were no more than 6 months old at enrollment. Referrals and coordination were not assessed because families were enrolling in home visiting at the same time they enrolled in MIHOPE, and therefore had not yet received any referrals or experienced coordination between programs.

Prenatal, Maternal, and Newborn Health

Although home visiting programs have historically emphasized the health and development of children, many recognize that a mother's physical and emotional health is intrinsically tied to the well-being of her children. Table 4.2 describes various aspects of the health of women and infants at the time they enrolled in the study, including their health status, health-related behaviors, and access to health care coverage.

Table 4.2. Selected Characteristics of Maternal, Prenatal, and Newborn Health, by Pregnancy Status at Enrollment

Characteristic (%)	Total	Women Who Enrolled During Pregnancy	Women Who Enrolled After Giving Birth
Maternal health, mental health, and well-being			
Health self-rated "poor" or "fair"	11.4	9.7	14.8 ***
Health problems self-rated as limiting activities "a lot"	18.7	20.9	13.9 ***
Depression (10-item CES-D) score at or above cutoff[a]	33.8	36.3	28.5 ***
Anxiety (GAD-7) score at or above cutoff[b]	25.2	28.4	18.6 ***
Prenatal health care			
Initiated prenatal care in the 1st trimester	79.7	79.3	80.6
Health-related behaviors			
Tobacco use			
Any tobacco use in the past 2 years	35.2	35.4	34.7
Any current smoking	15.2	12.3	21.3 ***
Smoking is permitted in the home	19.2	23.4	10.4 ***
Alcohol and substance abuse			
Binge alcohol use[c]	25.6	26.9	23.0 *
Illegal drug use[d]	12.9	14.6	9.3 ***
Maternal health insurance and access to care			
Insurance type[e]			
Uninsured	20.9	21.4	19.9

Characteristic (%)	Total	Women Who Enrolled During Pregnancy	Women Who Enrolled After Giving Birth
Public health coverage	70.9	70.9	70.8
Private insurance	12.1	10.6	15.3 ***
Has usual source of care[f]	62.9	58.1	73.0 ***
Birth outcomes			
Preterm birth (<37 weeks)	9.6	NA	9.6
Child had low birth weight, <2,500 grams or 5.5 lbs	10.5	NA	10.5
Child health care access			
Insurance type[e]			
Uninsured	12.0	NA	12.0
Medicaid/Children's Health Insurance Program (CHIP)	76.8	NA	76.8
Other	10.8	NA	10.8
Has usual source of primary care	93.4	NA	93.4
Sample size	1,652	1,119	533

Source: Calculations based on data from the MIHOPE family baseline survey.

Notes: NA = not applicable.

A chi-squared test was applied to differences between the characteristics of women who enrolled prenatally and women who enrolled postnatally, for categorical variables. A t-test was applied to differences in age between the women who enrolled prenatally and women who enrolled postnatally. Statistical significance levels are indicated as follows: *** = 1 percent, ** = 5 percent, * = 10 percent.

[a] This was measured using a 10-item Center for Epidemiologic Studies Depression Scale (CES-D). A score of 8 or higher indicates clinically significant depressive symptoms. See Kohout, Berkman, Evans, and Cornoni-Huntley (1993).

[b] A score of 10 or higher on the Generalized Anxiety Disorder seven-item scale (GAD-7) indicates moderate or severe anxiety symptoms. See Spitzer, Kroenke, Williams, and Löwe (2006).

[c] Binge alcohol use is defined as drinking four or more drinks in one sitting, and was reported for the three months before pregnancy.

[d] Illegal drug use was reported for the month prior to pregnancy.

[e] Insurance-type percentages may not add up to 100 percent, as some survey respondents indicated having more than one type of insurance.

[f] Maternal usual source of care includes all care except prenatal care and family planning.

One indicator of maternal health is a mother's own account of her health status. Although it is a subjective measure, longitudinal research studies have found that self-rated health status is a surprisingly strong predictor of future health deterioration and mortality, even after adjusting for objective measures of health.[44] Few women in MIHOPE reported they were in fair or poor health at the time they enrolled in the study, although women who had already given birth were more likely to do so. Not surprisingly, more pregnant women in MIHOPE than women who had already given birth faced limitations on engaging in moderate activities such as moving a table, vacuuming, or climbing several flights of stairs.

Improving prenatal health is an important objective of many home visiting programs. This goal could include reducing unhealthy behavior such as tobacco use, poor nutrition, and alcohol consumption, as well as ensuring early access to prenatal health care. The American College of Obstetrics and Gynecology recommends that prenatal care visits begin as soon as a woman knows she is pregnant. The vast majority of women in MIHOPE initiated prenatal care in the first trimester of pregnancy. Some initiated care before they enrolled in home visiting, suggesting that early initiation of prenatal care is already high among women in the MIHOPE sample.

Mothers and children can both benefit from reduced maternal tobacco, alcohol, and drug use. These behaviors are associated both with negative birth outcomes such as fetal growth retardation, and with risks for children after birth, such as respiratory illness, and in the case of alcoholism and illegal drug use, cognitive delays, child abuse and neglect, and intimate partner violence.[45] Home visiting may help families mitigate the prevalence or frequency of these behaviors, and families with histories of substance use and household tobacco use are identified as priority groups for MIECHV in the authorizing legislation.

Table 4.2 shows that about 35 percent of women reported using tobacco in the previous two years. Although this is much higher than the national rate of smoking among all adult women (16 percent) and the rate among pregnant women (12 percent),[46] it is similar to the smoking rate of female Medicaid enrollees prior to becoming pregnant (34 percent).[47] Pregnant women in MIHOPE were almost half as likely to smoke as women who had already given birth, but more than twice as likely to permit smoking in the house. Regarding substance use, few women reported using illegal drugs in the month prior to pregnancy, but a quarter of the sample reported an episode of binge drinking (consuming four or more drinks in a two-hour period) during the three months prior to pregnancy. However, frequent binge drinking was rare:

only 4 percent of those who reported binge drinking in the three months prior to pregnancy did so at least every other week. Since respondents tend to underreport the prevalence of these behaviors, the true rates of smoking and substance use are likely to have been higher than shown.[48]

In addition to physical health, home visiting programs are increasingly trying to address maternal mental health problems, as these problems can have serious repercussions for both maternal and child well-being.[49] Poor maternal mental health may also present different risks to pregnant women and their unborn children than it does to women who have already given birth and their infants. For example, maternal anxiety during pregnancy may harm fetal development by altering the uterine hormonal environment, which in turn impairs the central nervous system of the fetus and subsequent infant motor development, while maternal anxiety after giving birth may affect maternal parenting, which may consequently increase children's risk for anxiety disorders.[50]

There are high rates of depressive symptoms in the MIHOPE sample: About a third of women indicated such symptoms. This rate is much higher than the 13 percent of women who have depressive symptoms nationally while pregnant or soon after pregnancy.[51] However, depression may be substantially higher among low-income women with young children than among other income groups.[52] Perhaps for that reason, the prevalence rates of depressive symptoms among MIHOPE women are comparable to those found in smaller, community-based studies of low-income pregnant mothers.[53] More pregnant MIHOPE women than postpartum women expressed high levels of anxiety (28 percent compared with 19 percent). It is important to note that these are not clinical assessments of anxiety or depression, although validation studies have found that measures of depressive and anxiety symptoms are moderately to highly correlated with clinical diagnoses.[54]

Beyond health status, maternal access to health care at the time of enrollment is also relevant, as a wide body of research has documented that the uninsured receive fewer preventive and diagnostic services, and tend to be at a more severe stage of illness when they are diagnosed with a medical condition.[55] Lacking insurance coverage is a notable barrier to receiving adequate prenatal care, and may also prevent mothers from seeking health care for themselves after birth.[56] Lacking insurance coverage has also been linked to racial and ethnic differences in whether a person has a regular source of care.[57]

At the time of enrollment, about 71 percent of the women in MIHOPE reported receiving public health coverage, which includes Medicaid,

Medicare, Medigap, Children's Health Insurance Programs (CHIP), military insurance, the Indian Health Service, and state-sponsored insurance. The high rate of public health coverage reflects these women's low incomes. However, about one in five pregnant women and one in five new mothers were uninsured. The 15-month follow-up report may find higher rates of health coverage because of the provisions in the Affordable Care Act that expand coverage opportunities.

The majority of women had a usual source of care, although pregnant women were less likely to report this (58 percent compared with 73 percent). This may reflect the fact that pregnant women were asked not to consider prenatal care or family planning as their regular source of care, even though many of them might have been using prenatal care in that way.

Birth weight and gestational age are well-recognized measures of birth outcomes and infant health tracked and monitored by the Centers for Disease Control and Prevention. These newborn health indicators are also associated with long-term health and development and therefore serve as key characteristics to identify subgroups of children who are at particular risk of poor long-term outcomes. Table 4.2 shows that about 10 percent of the women who had given birth shortly before enrolling in MIHOPE had a preterm birth (an infant born at less than 37 weeks of gestational age), which is actually lower than the national average of 12 percent. Just over 10 percent reported having had a low-birth-weight infant, which is slightly higher than the national average of 8 percent.[58] Finally, 77 percent of children in MIHOPE were covered by Medicaid and CHIP, which is similar to the proportion of MIHOPE mothers with public health coverage. It is notable that 1 in 10 children lacked any type of insurance or health coverage when they enrolled in the study, given the number of federal, state, and local programs that provide low-cost or free health coverage for young, low-income children. Nevertheless, almost all mothers reported that their children had usual sources of care.

Child Health and Development and Parenting

To help parents improve their children's health and development, home visiting programs emphasize positive parenting skills. Table 4.3 describes the quality of the home environment as observed by a research team field interviewer at the time of enrollment into the study, as well as survey reports of characteristics that may foster or indicate positive parenting practices, including breastfeeding. This table also shows measures of father involvement, which is important given the growing literature on father involvement and its relationship to child well-being.[59]

Table 4.3. Selected Home Environment and Parenting Characteristics, by Pregnancy Status at Enrollment

Characteristic (%)	Total	Women Who Enrolled During Pregnancy	Women Who Enrolled After Giving Birth
Environment for learning[a]			
Mother has weak conversational skills[b]	12.0	11.8	12.5
Home is cluttered or unclean	15.1	14.2	16.9
Evidence of recent alcohol or drug use in the home	6.1	6.9	4.5*
Household has at least 10 books	52.0	49.9	56.1**
Father involvement			
Biological father is present in the home	42.2	38.9	49.1***
Father provides material support for child[c]	56.8	50.0	70.2***
Parenting			
Mother has weak empathy skills[d]	24.4	25.6	21.8*
Mother ever breastfed	77.1	NA	77.1
Mother intends to breastfeed	82.6	82.6	NA
Sample size	1,652	1,119	533

Sources: Calculations based on data from the MIHOPE family baseline survey and the research team's baseline home observations.

Notes: NA = not applicable.

A chisquared test was applied to differences between the characteristics of women who enrolled prenatally and women who enrolled postnatally, for categorical variables. A t-test was applied to differences in age between the women who enrolled prenatally and women who enrolled postnatally. Statistical significance levels are indicated as follows: *** = 1 percent, ** =5 percent, * = 10 percent.

[a] Based on observations of the home interior. These data are available for all families.

[b] This means that the mother's speech was not distinct, she did not initiate conversations, or she did not converse in a free and easily audible manner.

[c] Father helped with pregnancy expenses or bought things for the child a few times a month or more.

[d] Parental empathy for children's needs was measured using a subscale of the Adult Adolescent Parenting Inventory-2. See Bavolek and Keene (1999).

In some respects, most study participants had home environments that appeared to be conducive to fostering healthy child development. Only about 15 percent had cluttered or unclean homes, and evidence of recent alcohol or drug use was found in only a small minority of homes (6 percent). Most women exhibited adequate conversational skills, with only 12 percent observed to have weak skills (which means their speech was not distinct, they did not initiate conversations, or they did not converse in a free and easily audible manner). Weak conversational skills may indicate difficulties in promoting children's cognitive development.

However, only about half of all households in MIHOPE had at least 10 books, a measure that is correlated with family literacy practices and child language and cognitive development.[60]

Another way that women can support the healthy development of their children is to breastfeed. The bottom of Table 4.3 shows that most pregnant women intended to breast-feed and most women who had given birth had initiated breastfeeding. This is important because breast milk promotes the immunological health and growth of infants and may have health benefits for mothers.[61] These rates suggest that home visiting programs may not have to spend much time encouraging mothers to initiate breastfeeding. Nevertheless, there is room for home visiting to make a difference in longer-term breastfeeding rates, given that other community-based research studies have found that some low-income women who initiate breastfeeding do not continue past the first week.[62]

Only about 40 percent of women lived with the biological fathers of their children. This rate is similar to the rates of separate parental living arrangements found in the Fragile Families and Child Well-Being Study, a representative sample of births in urban hospitals from 1998 to 2000.[63] A recent review of the literature on family structure and child well-being has found that children of single mothers are at greater risk of poor health, behavioral, and cognitive outcomes. However, those poor child outcomes may be caused by mothers being in unstable relationships rather than mothers living separate from fathers per se.[64] In MIHOPE, more women who had already given birth than pregnant women were receiving material support from the father (70 percent compared with 50 percent). This difference may suggest that fathers become more involved after the births of their children.

Crime and Domestic Violence

Although most economically disadvantaged families are able to avoid violence and involvement with crime, the young children who are exposed to such events experience high levels of stress and are more likely to exhibit externalizing or "acting out" behavior later on.[65] Exposure to intimate partner violence is also associated with child abuse and neglect along with other adverse outcomes for children.[66] Table 4.4 presents several measures of criminal activity and intimate partner violence at the time women enrolled in the study.[67] About 7 percent of women reported that they had been arrested in the year prior to entering the study; this rate is slightly higher for women who enrolled during pregnancy. About 10 percent of women reported having experienced physical intimate partner violence and 7 percent reported having experienced psychological intimate partner violence in the past year. Roughly 21 percent of women who had already given birth and about 26 percent of pregnant women reported being physically violent to their spouses or partners in the previous year. However, the context in which this violence was experienced and perpetrated by women is unknown. Research has indicated that it is important to consider contextual factors when comparing the rates at which women are perpetrators or victims of violence. For example, women may perpetrate violence in self-defense, or as a coping mechanism for violence or other sources of stress.[68] Prior research has sometimes found that victimization and perpetration are related: For example, one study of women assessed for intimate partner violence in an emergency department setting found that 56 percent of victims had also perpetrated violence over the past year.[69] Two percent to 3 percent of women in MIHOPE reported perpetrating severe physical intimate partner violence (defined as using a knife, gun, or weapon or choking, slamming, kicking, burning, or beating one's partner) at least once in the prior year.

Intimate partner violence is not only a concern for adult victims; it also has consequences for children. Children of abused women are often victims of abuse and neglect themselves, and are apt to witness violent altercations between their parents.[70] Witnessing intimate partner violence has been shown to affect children's behavioral and health outcomes, leading to poor academic performance and higher rates of posttraumatic stress disorder, depression, anxiety, and substance use and abuse.[71] Male children who are exposed to intimate partner violence between their parents are more likely to engage in intimate partner violence as adults, and female children who witness intimate partner violence are more likely to enter into abusive relationships in adulthood.[72] Because home visitors have unique access into families' lives, they may have opportunities to prevent and address intimate partner violence by identifying its presence and by reaching socially isolated families who are disconnected from other service providers.

Table 4.4. Selected Characteristics of Crime and Intimate Partner Violence, by Pregnancy Status at Enrollment

Characteristic (%)	Total	Women Who Enrolled During Pregnancy	Women Who Enrolled After Giving Birth
Crime			
Arrests in the past year	7.3	8.2	5.3**
Intimate partner violence[a]			
Physical violence toward mother			
Any violence toward mother[b]	10.4	10.5	10.2
Severe violence toward mother[c]	2.3	2.2	2.4
Psychological violence toward mother[d]	7.0	6.7	7.8
Physical violence perpetrated by mother			
Any violence perpetrated by mother[b]	24.6	26.3	20.9**
Severe violence perpetrated by mother[c]	2.3	2.1	2.7
Sample size	1,652	1,119	533

Source: Calculations based on data from the MIHOPE family baseline survey.

Notes: A chi-squared test was applied to differences between the characteristics of women who enrolled prenatally and women who enrolled postnatally, for categorical variables. A t-test was applied to differences in age between the women who enrolled prenatally and women who enrolled postnatally. Statistical significance levels are indicated as follows: *** = 1 percent, ** = 5 percent, * = 10 percent.

[a] Only women with a spouse or partner living in the household at the time of enrollment were asked about experiences of intimate partner violence.

[b] Acts included in this measure are throwing something at one's spouse or partner; pushing, shoving, hitting, slapping, or grabbing one's spouse or partner; using a knife, gun, or weapon on one's spouse or partner; and choking, slamming, kicking, burning, or beating one's spouse or partner. Using threats of force to make her have sex is also included in the measure of any intimate partner violence toward the mother and is not included in the measure of any intimate partner violence perpetrated by the mother.

[c] Acts included in this measure are using a knife, gun, or weapon on one's spouse or partner, and choking, slamming, kicking, burning, or beating one's spouse or partner. Using threats of force to make her have sex is also included in the

measure of severe intimate partner violence toward the mother and is not included in the measure of any intimate partner violence perpetrated by the mother.

[d] This was measured using a six-item version of the Women's Experience with Battering scale. Smith, Earp, and DeVellis (1995), modified with the permission of Paige Smith.

Family Economic Self-Sufficiency

Family economic self-sufficiency was identified by the legislation that created MIECHV as a priority outcome for home visiting services. The importance of improving economic self-sufficiency is underscored by research documenting the numerous, negative consequences of poverty, including negative impacts on birth outcomes and child health, cognitive development, academic achievement, and social and emotional development.[73] Family economic characteristics may also be used to identify important subgroups high-lighted in the legislation, such as low-income families. Table 4.5 presents a number of indicators of family economic self-sufficiency, including maternal employment history, maternal earned income, household receipt of public benefits, and maternal education.

Although the majority of mothers had been employed at some point during the three years before they enrolled in MIHOPE, about 24 percent of pregnant women and 20 percent of other women had not. More than half of the sample reported no monthly earnings in the most recent month, which is not surprising given the sample's youth and how close its members were to a recent or upcoming birth. Turning to receipt of public benefits, 75 percent of mothers were enrolled in the Women, Infants, and Children program (WIC) at the time they joined the study. Similarly, the majority were enrolled in the Supplemental Nutrition Assistance Program (SNAP), and about half were enrolled in both WIC and SNAP (not shown). Overall, women who enrolled in MIHOPE after giving birth were more likely to have been receiving public benefits than pregnant women; in particular, the women who enrolled into the study after giving birth reported receiving SNAP, WIC, or earnings from other household members at higher rates than did pregnant women. While about 19 percent of the full sample reported house-hold receipt of disability insurance including Supplemental Security Income or Social Security Disability Insurance, more pregnant women (20 percent) reported household receipt of disability insurance (which may include short-term disability insurance related to pregnancy complications or conditions) than women who enrolled after birth (15 percent).

Table 4.5. Selected Economic Self-Sufficiency Characteristics, by Pregnancy Status at Enrollment

Characteristic (%)	Total	Women Who Enrolled During Pregnancy	Women Who Enrolled After Giving Birth
Maternal employment during the past three years			
None	22.3	23.7	19.5*
Employed for 1-12 months	38.0	39.9	34.2**
Employed for 13 months or more	39.6	36.4	46.4***
Household income in the last month			
Maternal monthly earnings			
$0	64.3	60.6	71.9***
$1 - $999	20.9	23.9	14.6***
$1,000 - $1,999	11.0	11.9	9.1
$2,000 or more	3.9	3.6	4.5
Sources of household income or benefits			
Temporary Assistance for Needy Families (TANF)	22.1	20.5	25.6**
Food stamps/SNAP	62.0	59.0	68.1***
Disability insurance	18.5	20.3	14.9***
Earnings from other household members	30.1	26.2	37.9***
WIC	75.3	70.7	85.1***
Maternal education			
Currently taking education or training classes	25.7	29.1	18.4***
Currently planning to take educationor training classes[a]	62.3	64.2	58.8*
Highest level of education[b]			
No high school diploma			
Age 20 and younger	22.0	26.3	12.8***
Age 21 and older	22.3	19.9	27.4***
High school diploma	33.6	33.7	33.3
Some college but no degree	16.4	14.8	19.7**
Bachelor's degree or higher	3.0	2.6	3.9
Sample size	1,652	1,119	533

Source: Calculations based on data from the MIHOPE family baseline survey.

Notes: A chi-squared test was applied to differences between the characteristics of women who enrolled prenatally and women who enrolled postnatally, for categorical variables.

A t-test was applied to differences in age between the women who enrolled prenatally and women who enrolled postnatally. Statistical significance levels are indicated as follows: *** = 1 percent, ** = 5 percent, * = 10 percent.

[a] Of the women who were not taking educational or training classes when they enrolled, the percentage who were planning to do so before their children's first birthdays.

[b] Does not include 2.7 percent of respondents who reported earning an associate's degree. Percentages may not add up to 100 as a result.

MIHOPE mothers also possessed low levels of education at the time they enrolled, which may reduce their ability to find jobs that pay well enough to make them economically self-sufficient. Only a small number (fewer than 3 percent) had obtained college degrees, for example, and more than 40 percent had no high school diploma. In comparison, most births in the United States occur among women with some college education or more (54 percent), while only 20 percent of births in the United States occur among women with less than a high school education.[74] In part, the low high school graduation rate may reflect the youth of the sample, but among women 21 and older, nearly 20 percent of pregnant women and 27 percent of other women had not graduated from high school. Women who enrolled in MIHOPE after giving birth were more likely than pregnant women to report that they had completed some college courses. At the same time, pregnant women were more likely to report that they were then taking or were planning to take educational or training classes.

Characteristics by National Model

As noted in the beginning of the section, each of the four national models defines its eligible population somewhat differently. For example, all programs can enroll pregnant women, but only Nurse-Family Partnership enrolls solely first-time, expectant mothers no later than the twenty-eighth week of pregnancy. Both Healthy Families America and Parents as Teachers allow local programs to select or refine their target populations to a certain extent (they can target, for example, families at risk of child maltreatment, families with low literacy levels, or families with mental health and substance-use issues), which implies that these programs may have a fair degree of variation in the risk profiles of families. Similarly, Early Head Start allows local programs flexibility in defining their target populations, but also specifies that eligible families should be at or below the federal poverty level, and further targets children with disabilities. Therefore, most Early Head Start families are expected to have low incomes and some might have children with special needs.

Table 4.6 presents selected baseline family characteristics across the four national models. This table highlights differences in risk factors and in primary reasons for enrolling in home visiting. Women who enrolled in one program may be demographically different from women who enrolled in another, and as a result may have different motivations and expectations.

Families vary as expected in the demographic characteristics that distinguish models' eligibility criteria. Nurse-Family Partnership programs enrolled only expectant mothers no later than the twenty-eighth week of pregnancy (although a few were at their twenty-eighth week and thus on the cusp of being ineligible), and women enrolled by Nurse-Family Partnership programs were consequently about twice as likely as women enrolled in any of the other programs to be pregnant. Although all models were reaching young pregnant mothers (under age 21), on average Nurse-Family Partnership programs had higher shares of this group, likely because that model only enrolls first-time mothers. In contrast, Early Head Start and Parents as Teachers programs were reaching more families with older children living in the home.

There appear to be few differences across the national models in the risk profiles of families. For example, there are no sizable differences in reports of substance abuse, mental health concerns, or prior maternal arrests across national models.

However, rates of living with biological fathers and of maternal education do vary across models: Women enrolled in Parents as Teachers were the least likely to be living with children's biological fathers at the time of enrollment and had the least education.

In recent years, there has been growing interest among members of the public health community in documenting the role of early life experiences in children's development, particularly exposure to stressful events, because these experiences could potentially harm children's long-term health and well-being.

The Adverse Childhood Experiences study used retrospective questionnaires of adults enrolled in a large health maintenance organization, collecting information on different categories of adverse childhood experiences including abuse (physical, sexual, or psychological), witnessing domestic violence against one's mother, living with substance abusers, living in households with mentally ill or suicidal individuals, and living with individuals who had been imprisoned.[75] By linking reports of adverse early life experiences to indicators of current health and well-being, the Adverse Childhood Experiences study demonstrated that as the number of negative experiences in childhood increases, the risk for a number of problems in adulthood (such as alcoholism and alcohol abuse, depression, poor health-related quality of life, illicit drug use, intimate partner violence, smoking, and unintended pregnancies) also increases.

Table 4.6. Selected Family Characteristics at Enrollment, by Program Model

Characteristic	Total	EHS	HFA	NFP	PAT
Maternal demographic and household characteristics					
Average age (years)	23.4	25.0	23.2	21.1	25.1***
Age 15-20 (%)	36.9	21.3	37.0	55.4	25.7***
Pregnancy status (%)					
Pregnant					
Less than 28 weeks	51.6	35.6	31.9	98.7	35.0***
More than 28 weeks	16.1	23.1	24.2	1.3	18.3***
Given birth	32.3	41.2	44.0	0.0	46.7***
Pregnant when enrolled and under 21 years old (%)	29.3	15.7	23.8	55.4	16.1***
Nonadult sibling of the child living in the home[a] (%)	34.2	58.6	34.6	1.3	54.8***
Risk factors (%)					
Maternal experience or perpetration of physical intimate partner violence	26.5	20.8	29.3	27.1	25.4
Maternal substance abuse[b]	33.0	30.4	32.8	34.6	32.7
Maternal mental health concerns[c]	40.9	40.5	41.8	42.3	38.9
Biological father who does not live in the household	57.8	59.1	57.3	62.9	52.8**
Low level of maternal education[d]	29.2	32.4	30.5	17.6	37.8***
Mother arrested in the past year	7.3	6.1	7.3	7.5	7.7
1 risk factor	28.9	33.3	28.3	25.6	30.8
2 or more risk factors	58.4	55.4	59.7	58.9	57.8

Table 4.6. (Continued)

Characteristic	Total	EHS	HFA	NFP	PAT
Primary reasons for enrolling in home visiting services[e] (%)					
Prenatal, maternal, and newborn health	10.4	4.4	8.2	21.5	4.6***
Child health and development	35.4	53.7	29.7	31.2	37.0***
Parenting support	28.4	27.8	30.4	25.8	29.0
Family economic self-sufficiency	5.0	5.4	5.2	2.7	6.8*
Referrals and service coordination	11.5	15.6	11.1	7.0	14.3***
General advice and support	38.6	25.4	43.4	45.4	33.1***
Sample size	1,652	216	521	455	460

Source: Calculations based on data from the MIHOPE family baseline survey.

Notes: A chi-squared test was applied to differences among characteristics for the home visiting program groups. Statistical significance levels are indicated as follows: *** = 1 percent, ** = 5 percent, * = 10 percent.

EHS = Early Head Start-Home Based Program Option, HFA = Healthy Families America, NFP = Nurse-Family Partnership, PAT = Parents as Teachers.

[a] Includes stepsiblings.

[b] Defined as either binge drinking in the three months prior to becoming pregnant or using illicit drugs in the month before becoming pregnant.

[c] Defined as scoring at or above the cutoff on either a 10-item CES-D measure of depression or the GAD-7 measure of anxiety.

[d] Based on the mother's highest level of education completed and her age.

[e] Mothers were asked to provide up to three reasons for enrolling in home visiting. Percentages may not add up to 100 as a result.

Table 4.6 also presents a child risk index (based on a mother's reports of current adverse experiences in her family) that includes intimate partner violence (experienced or perpetrated), maternal substance abuse, poor maternal mental health, parents living separately, low maternal education, and maternal arrests in the past year.[76] More than half of families across all models reported two or more of these risk factors, which suggests a high level of risk for poor outcomes among their children. These rates of two or more negative risk factors are similar across all four models.

Conclusion

MIHOPE has enrolled a group of young women with low levels of education; relatively high rates of smoking, drinking, and drug use; and worrying rates of depressive symptoms and intimate partner violence. Each of these indicators is a well-documented, independent risk for compromised infant health and child development.[77] At the same time, many of these risks are arguably alterable with access to appropriate resources and services, and with education and encouragement to change. These risk factors thus suggest important ways for home visiting programs to help families improve their circumstances early in their children's lives. Section 5 explores whether home visiting programs participating in MIHOPE are operating programs intended to ameliorate these risk factors.

SECTION 5. CHARACTERISTICS OF LOCAL HOME VISITING PROGRAMS

The diverse nature of the risks faced by families (portrayed in Section 4) underscores the challenges facing home visiting programs. These programs must address deep-seated social issues such as poverty while also encouraging individual behavioral change.[78] This section presents the first look at how local home visiting programs included in the Mother and Infant Home Visiting Program Evaluation (MIHOPE) plan and support the implementation of this critical work.

This section has two overarching goals. One is to provide an initial examination of how local home visiting programs participating in MIHOPE are planning and supporting implementation. In particular, are their infrastructure and planned services consistent with the expectations of the Maternal, Infant, and Early Childhood Home Visiting Program (MIECHV) as well as their respective national models? The other objective is to provide information about the degree to which local programs vary in their approaches, and the extent to which they differ from their national models. Some variation across local programs is to be expected, given the breadth of MIECHV's goals, the number of national models that are being used, the flexibility that some models allow local programs, and the differences in community contexts. However, this will be the first systematic information available about the ways MIECHV local programs vary in their priorities and the types of support they offer for implementation.

The section begins by describing components of local programs' planned services, including whom the programs intend to serve, what outcomes they intend to improve, what services they plan to deliver to achieve those improvements, and whom they intend to hire to deliver services. While the study is still collecting data on individual families' experiences in the program, understanding local programs' blueprints for service delivery is a first stage in understanding the outcomes they aim to affect. Because MIECHV promotes change in a large number of domains, a particularly important question concerns which of these domains local programs rank as higher or lower priorities, and whether these rankings vary from program to program. Variation of this kind could ultimately lead to variation in family outcomes.[79] Because variations in local programs are likely to be driven by differences in the histories, goals, and approaches of the national models, the section often presents and discusses information on local programs by national model.

The second part of the section describes aspects of local programs' implementation systems, the infrastructure they have in place to support staff members in carrying out the program's planned family services. Specifically, the section summarizes the programs' referral agreements with other community partners and the types of administrative support they use to monitor and facilitate implementation. Finally, the section provides reports from home visitors themselves about how well trained and equipped they feel to deliver services related to each outcome domain.

The data presented are drawn from several sources: semistructured interviews and surveys with the four national model developers, web-based surveys of 80 program managers conducted around the time their programs entered the study (between October 2012 and February 2014), and web-based surveys of 422 home visitors conducted around the same time.

Main Findings

- **Most local programs reported that they aimed to improve a broad range of family outcomes.** Most programs aimed to improve all major outcomes named by the MIECHV authorizing legislation, including maternal health and well-being, positive parenting, child health and development, and economic self-sufficiency. To do this some local programs had made a higher priority of some outcomes since MIECHV began, especially outcomes related to prenatal and maternal health.

- **The national model developers differ from one another in their priorities.** This is not surprising given their different histories. This variation is generally reflected in local program priorities, although local programs often made a high priority of outcome areas that their national models do not consider a high priority.
- **Local programs had appropriate infrastructures.** They appeared to possess the types of implementation infrastructure that MIECHV explicitly expects of them, including management information systems, continuous quality improvement procedures,[80] and connections to community services in each domain area.
- **Home visitors generally thought they were adequately trained.** The majority of home visitors reported that they were adequately trained and equipped to help mothers improve the full range of outcomes targeted by MIECHV. However, more of them perceived their training and tools to be adequate for outcomes related to child development and parenting than for outcomes related to maternal health and well-being.

Characteristics of Planned Home Visiting Services

This section describes what the four national models and the local programs involved in MIHOPE said about whom they intend to serve, which outcomes they intend to influence, what approaches they intend to take to delivering services, and how they intend to hire staff. The information is based on interviews with and materials from the national model developers and surveys of local program managers.

Intended Recipients

As discussed in Section 1, the four national models vary in the extent to which they target pregnant women. The national models also differ in which individuals within the family they aim to serve. Table 5.1 shows the family members for whom the national model developers and local programs report assuming "major responsibility" for improving out-comes.[81] The scope of perceived responsibility is potentially important because programs that assume major responsibility for affecting a greater number of family members may be more comprehensive, but may also be more challenging to implement because of their greater complexity.

As Table 5.1 shows, all four national models expect programs to assume major responsibility for the unborn or newborn child. Three of the four models also assume major responsibility for the mother (and the fourth assumes some responsibility for the mother, which is not shown in the table). In addition to the mother and child, Healthy Families America and Parents as Teachers also expect their local programs to assume major responsibility for the biological father. Parents as Teachers further expects local programs to assume major responsibility for other father figures and other children in the household (in addition to the unborn or newborn child).

Table 5.1. Individuals Targeted for Improved Outcomes, According to National Models and Local Programs

Major Responsibility Assumed for Individual	National Model Developer				Percentage of Local Programs				
	EHS	HFA	NFP	PAT	EHS	HFA	NFP	PAT	Overall
Child	Yes	Yes	Yes	Yes	100	96	89	84	93
Mother	-	Yes	Yes	Yes	61	88	100	84	84
Biological father	-	Yes	-	Yes	44	21	6	33	26
Other father figure	-	-	-	Yes	22	21	6	26	19
Other familial caregivers	-	-	-	-	22	4	6	22	13
Older children	-	-	-	Yes	11	0	0	11	5
Children born after the enrolled child	-	-	-	-	33	21	22	53	32
Sample size					18	24	19	19	80

Sources: Calculations based on data from the MIHOPE national model developer survey and the MIHOPE program manager baseline survey.

Note: EHS = Early Head Start-Home Based Program Option, HFA = Healthy Families America, NFP = Nurse-Family Partnership, PAT = Parents as Teachers.

The extent to which local programs' intended beneficiaries match the target populations described in their national models is a potential indicator of how well the national models' intentions are communicated to the local programs. This alignment between national and local offices' intentions may also influence the adequacy of the support available to help local programs achieve their goals. However, it is important to note that other factors, such as funders or other local organizations and partners, may influence a local program's intended beneficiaries. In general, the local programs were consistent with their national models. Nearly all local programs assumed major responsibility for the unborn or newborn child, most assumed major responsibility for the mother, and few assumed major responsibility for other family members. These results are consistent with prior research, which has found that typically only mothers and children participate in home visits. For example, one study of Healthy Families America found that fathers took part in only about 18 percent of visits, while a study of Early Head Start-Home Based Program Option found that only 17 percent of fathers participated in monthly home visits.[82]

Local programs also tended to vary in a pattern that is consistent with their national models. For example, the Early Head Start national office indicated that its programs are expected to assume some responsibility — but not major responsibility — for the mother, and Early Head Start local programs were the least likely of all MIHOPE programs to report assuming major responsibility for the mother. However, Early Head Start local programs were also the most likely to report major responsibility for the father, even though this was not a priority reported by the national Early Head Start office. Local program managers might have varied in these responses for reasons that are not related to the national models' priorities, reflecting, for example, the needs of the types of families they enroll in their programs, differing interpretations of what it means to assume major responsibility for an individual, and other influences on their programs such as MIECHV, local stakeholders, or other funders.

Goals and Intended Outcomes

As discussed in Section 1, both MIECHV and the national model developers may influence the outcomes that local programs emphasize. MIECHV expects states to change an ambitious range of outcomes, and local programs are expected to collect and report out-come data to the state in a number of different areas. At the same time, each of the national models also guides its local programs concerning specific program goals and outcomes, although some leave more discretion to local programs than others. In addition, local funders and other community-based agencies may exert an influence on the priorities of local programs, which may be especially relevant in MIHOPE since MIECHV funding is a relatively small share of local programs' overall funding streams (as described in Section 3).

Table 5.2 describes national model developers' and local program managers' priorities for outcomes in some of the domains specified in the MIECHV legislation. The extent to which the national model developers and local program managers agree on their priorities may indicate how clearly local programs will be able to communicate expectations to home visitors and how consistently they can prepare and support home visitors to fulfill these expectations. Clarity and consistency of support for specific outcomes may also affect how home visitors are trained and supported, the services they provide, and the outcomes they achieve.

As Table 5.2 shows, all four national model developers assign high priority (a ranking between 8 and 10 on a scale of 1 to 10) to five outcomes: promoting positive parenting behavior, preventing child abuse and neglect, fostering economic self-sufficiency, encouraging child preventive care, and promoting child development. However, the national model developers differ in how they rank other outcomes. Nurse-Family Partnership assigns high priority to all of the other eight outcomes, while Healthy Families America assigns high priority to all but four outcomes (prenatal health, maternal physical health, family planning and birth spacing,[83] and tobacco use). In comparison, Early Head Start assigns high priority to only one additional outcome (prenatal health). Parents as Teachers is the only national model developer to rank some outcomes as low priority (ranking between 1 and 3): maternal physical health, family planning and birth spacing, and tobacco use.

Despite these differences among the national model developers, a majority of local program managers ranked each outcome as a high priority. However, as was the case with intended recipients, there is some correspondence between the local and national rankings. For example, for four of the five outcomes that were rated high priorities by all national models, 95 percent or more of local programs also ranked them highly, and 83 percent of local programs rated the fifth such outcome (family economic self-sufficiency) as a high priority.

Likewise, where the national models diverge in their ranking of an outcome, there tend to be greater differences among local programs. For example, all local Nurse-Family Partnership programs rated family planning and birth spacing as a high priority, consistent with the national Nurse-Family Partnership rating. Meanwhile only 39 percent of Early Head Start programs and 42 percent of Parents as Teachers programs rated family planning and birth spacing as a high priority, consistent with their national model developers' reports that this outcome is a moderate (Early Head Start) or low priority (Parents as Teachers). Similarly, local programs varied along with their national models in how high a priority they made of intimate partner violence.

For particular maternal health outcomes, there appears to be disagreement between the national models and their respective local programs. For example, 59 percent to 71 percent of local Parents as Teachers and Early Head Start programs ranked maternal health and substance use as a high priority, whereas their national model developers ranked this as a moderate priority. Intimate partner violence was ranked as a moderate priority by the Early Head Start and Parents as Teachers model developers, but over 60 percent of local Early Head Start and Parents as Teachers programs rated this as a high priority.

Differences between national models and local programs could suggest that local programs are being tailored to local needs and concerns. These differences may also reflect the influences of MIECHV. As described earlier, local programs are expected to collect information on a number of benchmark indicators that state MIECHV agencies monitor. State agencies, in turn, are expected to show improvements on these indicators across funded programs in their states. State MIECHV administrators developed benchmark-data-collection plans articulating their planned approaches for collecting, analyzing, and reporting data for all constructs within the benchmark areas. State MIECHV administrators were given discretion to develop plans that reflected their programs' and populations' priorities, while adhering to federal and model developer requirements. Many grantees developed data working groups or advisory committees with representatives from local programs and other community organizations and agencies in various disciplines such as education, maternal and child health, child welfare, and law enforcement. These groups enabled grantees to build on the knowledge and expertise of a larger group of stakeholders to ensure that the benchmarks states chose were contextually and culturally appropriate. The groups also allowed grantees to link benchmark plans with other early childhood programs and initiatives in their states.[84]

Table 5.2. Priority Ratings for Intended Outcomes, by National Models and Local Programs

Outcome	National Model Developer Rating[a]				Percentage of Local Programs That Rated Outcome as a High Priority[b]				
	EHS	HFA	NFP	PAT	EHS	HFA	NFP	PAT	Overall
Maternal health and well-being									
Prenatal health	High	Medium	High	High	78	79	95	84	84
Maternal physical health	Medium	Medium	High	Low	47	63	74	63	62
Family planning and birth spacing	Medium	Medium	High	Low	39	79	100	42	66
Tobacco use	Medium	Medium	High	Low	35	78	84	42	62
Mental health and substance use	Medium	High	High	Medium	71	78	100	59	78
Intimate partner violence	Medium	High	High	Medium	67	92	100	61	81
Parenting									
Breastfeeding	Medium	High	High	Medium	72	78	94	58	76
Positive parenting behavior	High	High	High	High	100	92	100	100	97
Child abuse and neglect	High	High	High	High	100	100	100	89	98
Family economic self-sufficiency	High	High	High	High	78	88	89	74	83
Child health and development									
Birth outcomes	Medium	High	High	High	78	83	100	79	85
Child preventive care	High	High	High	High	100	96	95	89	95
Child development	High	High	High	High	100	96	100	95	98
Sample size					18	24	19	19	80

Sources: Calculations based on data from the MIHOPE national model developer survey and the MIHOPE program manager baseline survey.

Notes: EHS = Early Head Start-Home Based Program Option, HFA = Healthy Families America, NFP = Nurse-Family Partnership, PAT = Parents as Teachers.

[a] Low = ratings from 0 to 3, medium = ratings from 4 to 7, high = ratings from 8 to 10.

[b] High priority includes ratings of 8, 9, and 10.

The resulting benchmark indicators may go beyond the stated goals and priorities of the national model developers. In some cases, the addition of new priority areas for these established local programs implies that their planned services will grow more complex, meaning they will need to strengthen the training and support they provide to home visitors.

Table 5.3 shows the percentage of local program managers who reported that MIECHV changed how they rank different outcomes. No local program reported that MIECHV reduced the priority of an outcome. Thus, the table shows only whether program managers indicated that MIECHV increased their programs' focus on the outcome. About a third of Early Head Start programs reported raising the priority of various maternal health and well-being outcomes, as well as birth outcomes. Healthy Families America programs also reported increasing their emphasis on maternal health and well-being outcomes, particularly the outcomes of mental health and substance use and intimate partner violence. A small share of Nurse-Family Partnership programs reported raising the priority of outcomes related to mental health and substance use, intimate partner violence, parenting, and child health and development. It appears that local Parents as Teachers programs shifted the most after MIECHV, placing greater emphasis on a number of maternal health and well-being outcomes in particular. For example, more than half of local Parents as Teachers programs reported placing greater emphasis on family planning and birth spacing, tobacco use, and intimate partner violence.

Even if local programs ranked an outcome as a high priority, home visitors are the ones who must translate that priority into their daily work with families. Theories of behavior suggest that home visitors are more likely to help families in the outcome areas they believe they are expected to work on.[85] Table 5.4 displays the percentage of home visitors who agreed or strongly agreed that they were expected to help mothers achieve particular out-comes. The table shows that most home visitors, regardless of national model, believed that their role was to assist mothers with improving a wide range of outcomes. This is consistent with the local program managers' reports described in Table 5.3. For example, between 81 percent and 97 percent of home visitors (depending on the national model) agreed or strongly agreed that they were expected to help mothers have a healthy lifestyle during the prenatal period. Nearly all of the home visitors also reported that they were expected to assist mothers with behaviors to improve child health and development. Many also agreed that they were expected to help mothers become economically self-sufficient and gain access to relevant community resources for themselves, their children, or their families.

Table 5.3. Programs that Raised the Priority of Intended Outcomes as a Result of MIECHV

Outcome (%)	EHS	HFA	NFP	PAT	Overall
Maternal health and well-being					
Prenatal health	33	25	11	47	29
Maternal physical health	39	29	0	32	25
Family planning and birth spacing	33	29	5	53	30
Tobacco use	44	38	0	53	34
Mental health and substance use	33	42	16	47	35
Intimate partner violence	33	50	17	63	42
Parenting					
Breastfeeding	17	21	16	32	21
Positive parenting behavior	0	8	16	17	10
Child abuse and neglect	22	8	0	37	16
Family economic self-sufficiency	11	22	5	21	15
Child health and development					
Birth outcomes	39	17	11	33	24
Child preventive care	0	13	16	22	13
Child development	0	8	5	26	10
Sample size	18	24	19	19	80

Source: Calculations based on data from the MIHOPE program manager baseline survey.

Note: EHS = Early Head Start -Home Based Program Option, HFA = Healthy Families America, NFP = Nurse-Family Partnership, PAT = Parents as Teachers.

Table 5.4. Home Visitors' Perceptions of Their Role, by National Model

Home Visitors Are Expected to Help Mothers...[a] (%)	EHS	HFA	NFP	PAT	Overall
Maternal health and well-being					
Have a healthy lifestyle prenatally	81	91	97	88	90
Develop a healthy lifestyle outside of pregnancy	79	88	91	81	85
Space their births	48	80	89	60	71
Reduce their tobacco use	55	87	88	68	76
Recognize and deal with problem alcohol/other drug use	67	92	90	74	82
Recognize and deal with mental health issues	81	93	90	83	87

Home Visitors Are Expected to Help Mothers...[a] (%)	EHS	HFA	NFP	PAT	Overall
Recognize and address intimate partner violence	80	91	91	81	87
Parenting					
Start and continue breastfeeding	62	80	91	69	77
Use positive child behavior-management techniques	89	95	95	93	93
Babyproof their homes	84	95	88	92	90
Family economic self-sufficiency					
Become economically self-sufficient	72	89	91	68	81
Child health and development					
Make sure children are up-to-date on shots and well-child care	93	97	94	92	94
Support their children's cognitive and language development	92	97	96	95	95
Support their children's social and emotional development	92	97	96	95	95
Access to community resources					
Have health care coverage or access to a free or low-cost clinic for themselves	83	75	80	69	76
Secure high-quality child care	66	83	73	78	76
Have health care coverage or access to a free or low-cost clinic for their children	90	87	89	80	86
Get the public benefits for which they qualify	85	91	90	82	87
Sample size	87	130	118	105	440

Source: Calculations based on data from the MIHOPE home visitor baseline survey.

Notes: EHS = Early Head Start-Home Based Program Option, HFA = Healthy Families America, NFP = Nurse-Family Partnership, PAT = Parents as Teachers.

[a] Percentages reflect respondents who reported that they "agreed" or "strongly agreed."

Although expectations were high across all outcomes, the home visitor sample agreed on some more universally than others. Between 11 percent and 52 percent of home visitors, depending on the national model, did not agree that they were expected to help mothers improve birth spacing. Similarly, 12 percent to 45 percent of home visitors did not agree that they were expected to help mothers reduce their tobacco use.

Intended Service Delivery

The MIECHV authorizing legislation underscored the importance of adhering to a clear and consistent evidence-based home visiting model.[86] Core components of a local program's plans relate to the types and frequency of services that it delivers to clients. While information on actual service delivery is still being collected, it is important to ascertain first what services local programs intend to deliver to improve the family out-comes targeted by MIECHV, including those services' content, amount, and approach. Intended service delivery should influence actual service delivery and is the standard for measuring local programs' fidelity. This section describes programs' plans for service delivery and their alignment with programs' national models, and identifies early patterns of variation among local programs.

Table 5.5. Local Programs' Policies for Information Gathering, Education and Support, and Referrals

Program Policy (%)	Maternal Mental Health	Maternal Substance Use	Intimate Partner Violence	Parenting Behavior	Developmental Delays
Information gathering					
Formal screening is required[a]	95	72	71	77	99
At a specified time before or after a child's birth or enrollment[b]	91	70	71	77	99
When home visitor or parent has a concern[b]	42	19	22	15	55
Education and support[c]					
Family education and support when screening detects a problem					
Specified in written protocol[b]	35	23	23	26	54
Determined in consultation with supervisor[b]	53	31	34	32	39
Referral[c]					
Role of home visitor in making referral					
Provide information to families	33	49	42	37	27
Help family gain access to the resource	54	43	50	51	68
No policy	13	8	8	12	6
Role of home visitor in following through on referral					

Program Policy (%)	Maternal Mental Health	Maternal Substance Use	Intimate Partner Violence	Parenting Behavior	Developmental Delays
Home visitor expected to monitor	91	90	90	88	92
Home visitor not expected to monitor	0	0	2	0	3
No policy	9	10	8	12	6
Sample size					74

Source: Calculations based on data from the MIHOPE policies and procedures inventory.

Notes: [a] Possible screening tools included options for many commonly used tools, state-or model-specific tools, and respondent write-in options.

[b] Response categories are not mutually exclusive, so percentages can total more than 100. Within each domain, some sites might use more than one tool and might have different policies for each tool.

[c] Only for local programs where formal screening is required.

Content

Home visits consist of three types of tasks: information gathering, education and support, and referral to other services. Some programs may have formal policies or protocols concerning how to screen for different risks, and may provide explicit guidance on how to proceed when a problem is detected. Other programs may not have formal policies, or may allow home visitors more discretion to make decisions.

Table 5.5 displays the percentage of local programs with explicit policies for information gathering, education and support, and referral and follow-up for five outcome areas related to maternal health and well-being, parenting, and child development. The behavioral outcome areas described in Table 5.5 are assessed here because they reflect either important child outcomes or influences on child outcomes that all models endorse. In addition, identifying the presence of and need for services in these areas requires sensitivity and skill in gathering information and responding to results (in comparison with a more straightforward task such as screening a family for eligibility for a safety-net program). Finally, in each of these outcome areas valid and reliable screening tools exist that home visitors can readily use to identify needs and risks.

Nearly all local programs required formal screening of maternal mental health and infant developmental delays, but only about three-quarters required formal assessment of maternal substance abuse, intimate partner violence, and parenting behavior. This is consistent with the requirements of the national model developers, which all require local programs to conduct developmental screening but vary in their requirements for screening in other areas. Local programs varied somewhat by national model (see Appendix E). While nearly all Nurse-Family Partnership programs required formal screening for maternal substance use (consistent with a national model requirement), only a little over 60 percent of local Early Head Start and Parents as Teachers programs did. Nurse-Family Partnership programs were also more likely to require formal screening for intimate partner violence than the other local programs.

When a local program required a formal screening tool, it usually specified the timing of the screening rather than leaving it to the home visitor's discretion, although some local programs also allowed screening of maternal mental health and developmental delays whenever a home visitor or parent had concerns. This pattern is generally consistent across national models (see Appendix E).

Regarding education and support, all of the national models have requirements regarding programs' responses to screening results. These policies allow local programs to define specific standards and allow for staff members to make judgments regarding appropriate responses.

At the local level, Table 5.5 shows that many programs lacked protocols for education and support in response to positive screening results. About half had such written protocols for responding to developmental delays when they were found. However, only about 20 percent had written protocols for how to respond when a screen detected maternal substance use, intimate partner violence, or poor parenting behavior.

Local programs varied in whether they also required home visitors to consult with supervisors in deciding what to do in response to a positive screening result, perhaps in addition to having a written protocol. More than half required consultation with regard to maternal mental health. For the other outcomes, only 30 percent to 40 percent of local programs required home visitors to consult with their supervisors, and these proportions are largely the same across national models (see Appendix E).

Turning to referral policies, between 27 percent and 49 percent of local programs reported that home visitors were to provide information when making referrals to address problems revealed by screening, but that it was the family's responsibility to follow through. A greater percentage of local programs reported that home visitors were expected to help families gain access to necessary resources, for example by calling to arrange appointments or monitoring the outcomes of referrals. This pattern is consistent across the five outcome areas examined, with programs most likely to report that they expect home visitors to help families in response to developmental delays. It is also consistent with national model requirements that home visitors monitor families' success in using referrals. However, in each outcome area a handful of local programs had no policy on home visitors' role in making and following through on referrals.

Dosage

The number of home visits, or "dosage," that families are meant to receive is one aspect of service delivery for which all the national models provide guidance to their local affiliates. The national models vary in how they specify the duration and frequency of home visiting services. Home visits can last a minimum of 60 minutes (Parents as Teachers) to a minimum of 90 minutes (Early Head Start). All models establish either a minimum number of home visits per year or vary visits depending on the time since a family's enrollment or a child's age. Services can begin as early as pregnancy for all models, and depending on the model can be delivered until a child reaches age 2 (for Nurse-Family Partnership) to as much as age 5 (Healthy Families America). Local programs operating Healthy Families America and Parents as Teachers determine the length and intensity of services based on family need, and NurseFamily Partnership allows for adjustment of visit schedules to meet client needs. Nearly all local programs aligned with their national models in defining intended service initiation, duration, visit length, and visit frequency. For example, 89 percent of local programs reported that they had the same preference for visit length as their national model developers (results not shown).

Approach

It is clear that improving parenting and early child development are primary goals for all four national models. The approaches that home visitors use in their daily work with families are likely to influence their ability to achieve these goals. For example, a recent meta-analysis found that when parent training programs encourage parents to practice newly developed skills or techniques with their own children during program sessions, they produce significantly larger impacts on parenting behavior and child acting-out behaviors.[87] Table 5.6 therefore summarizes national and local approaches to specific parent-training techniques and supportive strategies including problem solving, modeling, and education.

Table 5.6. Parent Training Techniques and Supportive Strategies Encouraged by National Models and Local Programs

Technique or Strategy	National Model Developer[a]				Percentage of Local Programs That Encouraged Technique				
	EHS	HFA	NFP	PAT	EHS	HFA	NFP	PAT	Overall
Parent training techniques									
Demonstrating positive parenting practices	E	D	E	D	94	96	89	100	95
Directing parent-child activities	E	E	E	D	61	96	24	89	70
Observing and giving positive feedback on parent-child interaction	E	E	E	E	100	100	100	100	100
Observing and giving constructive feedback on parent-child interaction (noting ways parent could improve his or her behavior)	E	E	E	E	78	96	68	100	86
Playing with child/direct interaction with child	E	N	E	N	67	88	58	67	71
Supportive strategies									
Caregiver goal setting	E	E	E	E	94	100	100	100	99
Caregiver problem solving	E	E	E	E	94	100	100	100	99
Crisis intervention	E	E	E	N	78	83	79	95	84
Emotional support	E	E	E	E	94	100	95	95	96
Sample size					18	24	19	19	80

Sources: Calculations based on data from the MIHOPE national model developer survey and the MIHOPE program manager baseline survey.

Notes: EHS = Early Head Start-Home Based Program Option, HFA = Healthy Families America, NFP = Nurse-Family Partnership, PAT = Parents as Teachers.

[a] E = encouraged, D = discouraged, N = neither encouraged nor discouraged.

The table shows that all of the national models encourage home visitors to observe and provide parents with both positive and constructive feedback on their interactions with their children, and all of the national models encourage home visitors to use at least one supportive strategy such as goal setting, problem solving, or emotional support. In other respects, however, the national models differ. For example, both Healthy Families America and Parents as Teachers discourage home visitors from modeling (demonstrating) positive parenting practices, while Early Head Start and Nurse-Family Partnership encourage them to.[88] While Early Head Start, Healthy Families America, and Nurse-Family Partnership encourage home visitors to facilitate and guide parent-child activities, Parents as Teachers discourages this practice.

In contrast to their national models, most local programs across all national models reported that they encouraged the use of every technique shown in Table 5.6. The most prominent exception is that only 24 percent of local Nurse-Family Partnership programs encouraged home visitors to direct parent-child activities, even though the national model developer encourages this technique.

Intended Staffing

In order to provide high-quality services to families, programs must be adequately staffed. Two indicators of intended staffing include supervisor caseloads of home visitors and home visitor caseloads of families. Caseloads are important because they have been shown to be related to staff burnout and service quality.[89]

The national models vary in whether and how they specify limits for home visitor and family caseloads. Early Head Start does not have a policy specifying the number of home visitors a supervisor is to oversee. The other three models specify caseloads ranging from 6 (Healthy Families America) to 8 (Nurse-Family Partnership) to 12 (Parents as Teachers) home visitors per supervisor. Early Head Start and Nurse-Family Partnership have set family caseload limits for home visitors: Early Head Start specifies 12 families per home visitor and Nurse-Family Partnership specifies 25 families per home visitor. Healthy Families America and Parents as Teachers have more nuanced caseload limits. For example, Healthy Families America takes the frequency of visits into consideration when determining caseload size and Parents as Teachers sets different goals for numbers of home visits depending on the home visitor's years of experience and on whether or not the home visitor is working full time.

Most local programs have the same policies as their national models for the maximum number of home visitors a supervisor is expected to oversee (see Appendix E). As for number of families per home visitor, about 40 percent of local programs set their caseload limits lower than their national models, and about 60 percent of programs have caseload policies that are the same as the maximums specified by their national model developers.

Characteristics of Implementation Systems

Local programs' implementation systems consist of the infrastructure they have in place to prepare, enable, and reinforce staff members in carrying out their roles. The implementation system is the critical link between the local program's planned and actual service delivery. It includes system support, administrative support, staff recruitment, staff development, and clinical support.

System Support: Links and Referrals to Community Resources

MIECHV emphasizes home visiting's role as part of a larger early childhood system of care, specifically its role in improving coordination with and referrals to other community resources. Home visiting programs must work with other organizations to identify and reach eligible families and to connect enrolled families with services they need. It is possible that local programs with strong ties to other services may be more likely to get referrals from those organizations to help them fill available slots and enroll families likely to benefit from home visiting. Similarly, local programs with strong ties to community resources may be more successful at linking families to these services in order to improve outcomes.

One sign that a home visiting program has strong relationships with other local organizations is if it has formal referral agreements with them (memoranda of understanding, for example). Table 5.7 presents the percentage of local programs that have formal referral agreements with a range of local organizations that commonly refer families to home visiting programs. Overall, two-thirds of local programs have such agreements. Local programs without formal referral agreements may have informal arrangements for referrals or rely on other methods of recruitment such as direct outreach and walkins, although MIHOPE does not have systematic data on this. Healthy Families America programs were most likely to have written referral agreements; this may be due in part to the high percentage that reported having formal agreements with centralized intake systems. In many communities, a centralized intake system allows referrals to flow through one agency and then be assigned to the most appropriate service provider. More than half of Parents as Teachers programs also had formal arrangements with a centralized intake system.

Table 5.7. Formal Agreements with Referral Sources for the Recruitment of Families Across Local Programs

Referral Partner (%)	Local Programs with Formal Referral Agreements[a]				
	EHS	HFA	NFP	PAT	Overall
Any organization	72	79	47	63	66
Centralized intake	33	63	16	56	43
Maternal health and well-being					
Hospitals	11	38	11	22	22
Health departments	28	13	5	22	16
Prenatal clinics	22	13	21	17	18
Parenting					
Child welfare agencies	39	17	16	6	19
Family economic self-sufficiency					
WIC programs	28	38	16	22	27
Schools	33	21	5	22	20
Child health and development					
Pediatric clinics	28	8	5	6	11
Other[b]	17	4	16	0	9
Sample size	18	24	19	19	80

Source: Calculations based on data from the MIHOPE program manager baseline survey.

Notes: EHS = Early Head Start-Home Based Program Option, HFA = Healthy Families America, NFP = Nurse-Family Partnership, PAT = Parents as Teachers.

[a] Response categories are not mutually exclusive so percentages might total more than 100.

[b] Includes children and youth services, early intervention services, homeless services, juvenile delinquent halls, residential drug treatment programs, domestic violence shelters, and nonprofit community partners.

Aside from centralized intake systems, local programs had low rates of formal agreements with referral sources, ranging from the 27 percent that had formal agreements with Women, Infants, and Children (WIC) programs to the 11 percent that had formal agreements with pediatric clinics.

Home visiting programs do not assume that they can meet all of their clients' needs, so they depend on strong ties with other community providers for additional services. To assess the availability of services, local programs were asked to identify at least one provider to which they referred families for each of nine services relevant for MIECHV outcomes: prenatal care, family planning and reproductive health, substance use and mental health treatment, shelter from intimate partner violence, intimate partner violence counseling, adult education or employment services, pediatric primary care, child care, and early intervention services for babies and toddlers with developmental delays and disabilities. Nearly all local programs could identify at least one community resource to which they could refer enrolled families for each of the nine services. While this finding is encouraging, the existence of a service is just one indicator of its actual availability to the clients of the home visiting programs; future reports will use additional measures to assess these services' accessibility.

Administrative Support

MIECHV emphasizes that it is important for states to build the administrative support structures programs need to help them deliver intended services — management information systems, for example. It also calls for states to engage in continuous quality improvement — which includes practices to collect information used to monitor and provide feedback on program performance — and stipulates that training and technical assistance for these activities should be provided. Administrative support should promote fidelity in helping local programs carry out activities. For example, a program with a management information system to document and monitor service delivery might be more likely to deliver services successfully.

Table 5.8 describes the availability and use of three types of administrative support: management information systems, program monitoring, and continuous quality improvement activities. Overall, nearly all local programs reported using a management information system. In fact, over a quarter used more than one such system (not shown in the table), which might include both national and local systems. Similarly, nearly all local programs used their systems for internal program monitoring and quality improvement. Nearly three-quarters of local programs reported having designated staff members to assist with data entry.

Table 5.8. Data Management, Program Monitoring, and Continuous Quality Improvement Across Local Programs

Activity	Percentage of Local Programs
Data management	
Management information system (MIS) in place	99
Use of MIS for program monitoring and quality improvement	93
Staff to assist with service-delivery data entry	72
Program monitoring	
Annual or biannual reporting on local program performance	84
Monitoring of selected aspects of operations [a]	
Referrals into program	
Number of referrals	98
Appropriateness of referrals	75
Family enrollment	
Family retention rates at specific points	84
Reasons families drop out	89
Visits	
Visit frequency	99
Visit length	71
Mother no-show rates	68
Screening	
Maternal depression	76
Maternal substance use	54
Intimate partner violence	59
Child development	95
Continuous Quality Improvement (CQI)	
One or more CQI activities in the past 12 months	84
Staff members with dedicated time for CQI	62
Sample size	80

Source: Calculations based on data from the MIHOPE program manager baseline survey.

Note: [a] Response categories are not mutually exclusive so percentages might total more than 100.

Overall, the majority of local programs reported that they monitored many types of activities, but they varied in the scope of activities they monitored.

Nearly all monitored the number of referrals they received, and most monitored the appropriateness of these referrals. Nearly all monitored retention rates, the reasons families dropped out, and visit frequency, while a substantial majority monitored visit length and the frequency with which mothers failed to attend scheduled home visits

Local programs did vary in their monitoring of screening rates — not surprising, given how much variation there was among them in the type of screening they conducted. Nearly all monitored child-development screening rates, while a majority monitored screening rates for maternal depression, domestic violence, and maternal substance use. This pattern seems to be consistent with the priority given to these outcomes by the MIECHV benchmarks, national models, local program managers, and home visitors. Activities to improve the highest-priority outcomes (in this case, child development) were more likely to be monitored and have adequate administrative support.

Table 5.9. Availability of Consultants by Service Area Across Local Programs

Consultant Service Area (%)	Local Programs with Available Consultants				
	EHS	**HFA**	**NFP**	**PAT**	**Overall**
Any	100	63	79	53	73
Maternal health and well-being					
Prenatal health	94	63	74	53	70
Maternal physical health	94	63	74	53	70
Substance use	89	54	74	47	65
Stress and mental health	100	58	79	53	71
Healthy adult relationships	89	63	68	53	68
Family economic self-sufficiency	83	58	74	53	66
Child health and development					
Parenting to support child development	94	63	68	53	69
Parenting to support child health	94	58	74	53	69
Sample size	18	24	19	19	80

Source: Calculations based on data from the MIHOPE program manager baseline survey.

Note: EHS = Early Head Start -Home Based Program Option, HFA = Healthy Families America, NFP = Nurse-Family Partnership, PAT = Parents as Teachers.

Turning to continuous quality improvement, over 80 percent of local programs reported that they had undertaken such activities in the previous year. In addition, over 60 percent of local programs reported having a staff person with dedicated time to design and direct these activities, to collect information on them, and to analyze that information.

Clinical Support

Clinical support includes access to expert consultants as well as tools and strategies for providing services effectively. One key question related to clinical support is whether home visitors have access to expert consultants to help them address issues or situations beyond their skills and expertise. Prior work has found that consultative expertise in content areas is associated with stronger program implementation.[90] In a home visiting program, a consultant is typically a trained professional within or outside the local program's implementing agency who advises the home visitor about her work with individual families, although in some cases a consultant may go with a home visitor to a client's home.

Table 5.9 describes the availability of consultants across MIECHV outcome domains for local programs in each national model. Overall, most local programs reported access to expert consultants, and at least two-thirds reported providing access to consultants for each outcome domain. This varies considerably by national model, however. All Early Head Start local programs reported having access to at least one professional consultant and more than 80 percent of Early Head Start programs had access to consultants in each domain. This may be because most Early Head Start programs are based in large Head Start agencies, which typically employ other professionals including nurses and mental health counselors. In contrast, nearly half of Parents as Teachers programs did not have access to any consultants.

It is important to understand not only whether program managers believe that they have made clinical support available (as shown in Table 5.9), but also to get a sense of how home visitors perceive the value of this support, as well as the value of other strategies and tools provided by the program. Table 5.10 shows the percentages of home visitors who agreed or strongly agreed that their local programs provided useful strategies and tools to assist them in helping mothers achieve intended outcomes.

Among home visitors who reported that they were expected to assist mothers with particular outcomes, most agreed that their programs provided them useful strategies and tools to help mothers in those areas. However, in the areas of recognizing and dealing with problem substance use and mental health, about a quarter of home visitors (27 percent and 23 percent, respectively) did not agree that their programs provided them with useful strategies and tools to help mothers. More home visitors reported that their programs had useful strategies and tools to help them promote child health and development than outcomes in any other area, which is consistent with other results in this section relating to programs' attention to this domain.

Table 5.10. Home Visitors' Perceptions of the Usefulness of Their Programs' Strategies and Tools and the Adequacy of Their Training

Home Visitor Perception (%)	"Local Program Has Useful Strategies and Tools to Help Mothers..."[a]	"Home Visitors Are Adequately Trained to Help Mothers..."[a]
Maternal health and well-being		
Have a healthy lifestyle prenatally	91	90
Develop a healthy lifestyle outside of pregnancy	89	89
Space their births	82	84
Reduce their tobacco use	82	77
Recognize and deal with problem alcohol or other drug use	73	69
Recognize and deal with mental health issues	77	73
Recognize and address intimate partner violence	79	77
Parenting		
Start and continue breastfeeding	90	89
Use positive child behavior management techniques	91	90
Babyproof their homes	89	91
Family economic self-sufficiency		
Become economically self-sufficient	81	79
Child health and development		
Make sure children are up-to-date on shots and well-child care	92	94
Support their children's cognitive and language development	95	93

Home Visitor Perception (%)	"Local Program Has Useful Strategies and Tools to Help Mothers..."[a]	"Home Visitors Are Adequately Trained to Help Mothers..."[a]
Support their children's social and emotional development	95	93
Access to community resources		
Have health care coverage or access to a free or low-cost clinic for themselves	92	73
Secure high-quality child care	82	85
Have health care coverage or access to a free or low-cost clinic for their children	92	72
Get the public benefits for which they qualify	82	79
Sample size	NA[b]	NA[b]

Source: Calculations based on data from the MIHOPE baseline home visitor survey.

Notes: [a] Home visitors included are only those expected to help mothers with each activity. Percentages reflect respondents who reported that they "agreed" or "strongly agreed."

[b] NA = not applicable. Sample size varies for each variable. The percentage of home visitors expected to help mothers with each activity is shown in Table 5.4.

Staff Development

Each of the national models has specific approaches to initial and continuing training for its home visitors. Healthy Families America home visitors are required to receive orientation training prior to providing any services to families; role-specific core training within 6 months of being hired; continuing training within 3, 6, and 12 months of being hired; and annual training thereafter. All Early Head Start home visitors receive orientation training that focuses on the goals, philosophy, and implementation of the model. All home visitors are required to receive a minimum of 15 hours of continuing training, and are required to receive training in the curriculum and assessments used by the program. Parents as Teachers home visitors are required to attend a three-day foundational training course and a two-day model implementation training course prior to serving families. In addition, Parents as Teachers home visitors are required to complete 20 hours of professional development within one year of completing the model training, 15 hours during their second year, and 10 hours in their third and subsequent years. Nurse-Family Partnership home visitors are required to attend a self-directed training session and four days of inperson training prior to serving families. In addition, they must complete three online lessons within 6 months of the inperson training.

But requirements related to training do not reveal whether the training is helpful to home visitors, who must apply what they learn to meet both program and family goals. Table 5.10 presents the percentages of home visitors who agreed or strongly agreed that they had received adequate training to carry out their roles in helping mothers achieve particular outcomes. Among the home visitors who reported that they were expected to help mothers improve each outcome, a substantial majority felt they were adequately trained to help mothers in that area. Although the majority felt adequately trained to improve the wide range of outcomes related to maternal health and well-being and to help mothers with their children's health and development, about 30 percent of home visitors did not feel adequately trained to recognize and deal with substance use and mental health problems.

Conclusion

The results presented here suggest that local programs are setting up their MIECHV-funded home visiting programs in ways that are broadly consistent with expectations laid out in the legislation that created MIECHV, and that MIECHV is influencing how local programs set their priorities. Local programs have increased the priority of some outcomes identified as important in the MIECHV legislation, and are conducting the types of activities endorsed by the legislation, monitoring them in the ways it envisioned, and ensuring clinical support and training as it directed.

Each national model developer also exerts substantial influence over local programs: Local programs' reported priorities for family outcomes and approaches to service delivery tend to differ depending on the national model that they are implementing.

Across outcome domains, this section finds that the national models, local programs, and local staff members give the highest priority and the most support to activities related to child health and development and promoting positive parenting. There is more variation in the emphasis they place on activities related to maternal health and well-being; some outcome areas (for example, birth spacing, maternal physical health, tobacco use, and maternal mental health) are not uniformly ranked as a high priority by the national models or the local programs. Perhaps reflecting these differing priorities, fewer home visiting staff members report that they are expected to influence these outcomes than the outcomes related to child health and development and parenting, or report that they feel adequately trained or supported to influence them.

SECTION 6. DISCUSSION

This report to Congress provides an analysis of the states' needs assessments and initial plans for implementing home visiting programs funded under MIECHV. It also presents information available to date on the families, staff members, local programs, and national models participating in the Mother and Infant Home Visiting Program Evaluation (MIHOPE) and lays the foundation for future reports on the impacts and implementation of home visiting programs in MIHOPE. This section summarizes the report from these two perspectives.

Summary of Findings

The findings provide an early indication that MIECHV is being implemented in ways that support its intended goals. First, states developed plans to spend MIECHV funds in at-risk communities, as intended. They targeted counties with higher rates of poverty and child maltreatment than their respective averages, and with somewhat higher rates of premature birth. These differences are important because among MIECHV's stated goals are increasing family economic well-being, reducing child maltreatment, and improving birth outcomes.

In their initial plans, states indicated they would use MIECHV funds to support six evidence-based national models: Healthy Steps and Home Instruction for Parents of Pre-school Youngsters plus the four studied in MIHOPE: Early Head Start-Home Based Program Option, Healthy Families America, Nurse-Family Partnership, and Parents as Teachers. Of the 554 counties identified in initial state plans as recipients of MIECHV funds, 94 percent were implementing or planning to implement one of the four evidence-based models included in MIHOPE. These included 49 counties with Early Head Start programs, 177 local Healthy Families America programs, 169 local

Nurse-Family Partnership programs, and 123 local Parents as Teachers programs.

Interviews with MIECHV administrators in the 12 MIHOPE states reveal that they used the needs assessments to decide which communities to target and used research evidence from the Home Visiting Evidence of Effectiveness review to decide which evidence-based models to fund. Once these decisions were made, state administrators often deferred to local programs and the national models to set priorities among families at the community level.

MIHOPE sought to enroll about 85 local MIECHV-funded home visiting programs. States were required to participate if chosen and were expected to pass this mandate on to MIECHV-funded programs, but not every MIECHV-funded program was considered for the study. First, the study included only programs that had been in operation for two or more years in order to focus on those that had had a chance to mature to full effectiveness. Second, to conserve resources and to allow for the ethical creation of a control group, MIHOPE sought local programs that could contribute 40 or more families to the study over a period of about 18 months. Because programs in small communities often had difficulty meeting these two criteria, most MIHOPE sites are in metropolitan areas. Finally, to allow the study to separate the effects of geography from the effects of program models, MIHOPE sought to include states that used MIECHV funds to expand at least two of the four national models selected by at least 10 states. This criterion excluded most states. Taken together, therefore, the local programs included in MIHOPE are more urban and more mature than the full set of programs listed in the initial state plans. However, the 12 MIHOPE states include some of the largest states in the country and did receive about a third of all MIECHV funds, so they are indicative of a large number of MIECHV-funded programs.

Even if they are not completely representative of MIECHV programs nationally, the local programs included in MIHOPE serve a very disadvantaged group of mothers. When they entered the study, more than 30 percent had symptoms of depression; almost 20 percent had health problems that limited their activities; most were receiving some form of public assistance from sources such as the Supplemental Nutritional Assistance Program, Temporary Assistance for Needy Families, or disability benefits; more than three-quarters had no more than a high school diploma; and about a tenth had been the victim of intimate partner violence. Of babies born to mothers prior to entering the study, about 10 percent were born prematurely and nearly 11 percent had low birth weights. MIHOPE should therefore provide a good test of how these models affect the families the authorizing legislation aimed to reach.

Fortunately, MIECHV-funded programs are designed to be able to help families overcome the multiple and severe problems they face. Home visitors reported that they were expected to help families achieve better outcomes in all the areas specified in the authorizing legislation and to overcome a large number of risk factors. Home visitors also mostly reported that they were well trained and supported in helping families address a wide range of issues. In addition, local programs reported making a high priority of out-comes in the domains mentioned in the legislation. The final report from the implementation study will provide information on the frequency and content of training and supervision for home visitors, the amounts and types of services provided to individual families in the study, the ways services vary for families with different risk factors, and the implementation factors related to stronger service delivery at the local level.

Implications for Future Reports

In addition to providing the first glimpse of how MIECHV is being implemented by states and local home visiting programs, this report lays the groundwork for future MIHOPE analyses. In the coming years, MIHOPE plans to draw on additional data to issue findings in three areas: (1) local program implementation (including the costs of operating the programs), (2) the estimated effects of home visiting programs in each domain specified in the authorizing legislation, and (3) the features of local programs that are associated with larger or smaller effects for families.

The characteristics of the families in the study shed some light on which subgroups could be reliably examined. Of the high-priority groups listed in the legislation that created MIECHV, MIHOPE is well positioned to learn about low-income families, which are the target of all four national models; pregnant women under age 21, who make up 37 percent of the MIHOPE sample so far; substance users (33 percent); and families where tobacco is used (36 percent).[91] MIHOPE will also be able to address additional questions concerning whom the programs benefit. For example, it will be able to address how program services and effects vary with mothers' depressive symptoms, whether programs are more effective if women enroll earlier in pregnancy, and how services vary by national model.

Section 5 also presents several contrasts in program implementation that can be explored in future analyses, including the extent to which programs focus services on different outcomes and the impacts they achieve, differences among the national models, and differences between the goals articulated by national model developers and the actual implementation plans of local programs. Here are some examples of hypotheses generated by these contrasts:

- Do programs provide families with services aimed at achieving the outcomes identified in the authorizing legislation? This report indicated that local programs have modified their goals to address outcomes specified by the MIECHV authorizing legislation and that they have infrastructure in place to help families achieve these outcomes. However, the current report cannot provide information on whether these goals and infrastructure lead to services that are appropriate for the particular families being served. A future MIHOPE report on program implementation will explore that issue.
- Do families benefit more when home visiting programs make a high priority of a wide range of outcomes, or when they focus on a narrower set of outcomes? All four national models indicated that they give the highest priority to five outcome domains: positive parenting practices, child abuse and neglect, economic self-sufficiency, child preventive care, and child development. Both Nurse-Family Partnership and Healthy Families America consider several other areas to be high priorities as well. In contrast, the national Early Head Start and Parents as Teachers offices placed less emphasis on maternal health (other than prenatal care), health behaviors such as smoking, and some other outcomes. To the extent that the national models can help local programs achieve all of their goals, impacts for Nurse-Family Partnership and Healthy Families America should be spread widely across outcome domains. In comparison, the more focused approach advocated by Early Head Start and Parents as Teachers nationally may allow local programs running those models to put more resources into parenting and child outcomes, resulting in larger effects in those areas than are achieved by programs running Nurse-Family Partnership and Healthy Families America.
- Does allowing local sites discretion in whom they serve and how they provide services result in more or less effective local programs? Nurse-Family Partnership's national office provides precise guidance

to local programs on whom they should enroll, the qualifications home visitors should have, and the curricula they should use, and it closely monitors the programs to make sure they comply with model requirements. In contrast, Early Head Start, Healthy Families America, and Parents as Teachers all allow local programs more discretion in whom they serve and how they provide services. MIHOPE will explore whether programs with more discretion are better able to adapt to the needs of the families they serve (thus producing larger benefits to families) or whether they provide more widely variable services because staff members are not given either the clear guidance or the tools to support their work they might receive under a more prescriptive model.

This report indicates that MIECHV-funded home visiting programs serve a disadvantaged but varied group of families using service delivery strategies that also vary across programs. MIHOPE will aim to shed light on questions regarding the relationships among family risk factors, service delivery strategies, program costs, and program impacts. In so doing, the study will build on its rigorous research design to provide lessons for the MIECHV program and the home visiting field as they continue to look for new ways to improve outcomes for children and families in disadvantaged communities across the country.

REFERENCES

Aber, J. Lawrence., Neil G. Bennett., Dalton C. Conley. & Jiali, Li. (1997). "The Effects of Poverty on Child Health and Development." *Annual Review of Public Health*, 18, *1*, 463-483.

Abraído-Lanza, Ana F., Adria, N. Armbrister., Karen, R. Flórez. & Alejandra, N. Aguirre. (2006). "Toward a Theory-Driven Model of Acculturation in Public Health Research." *American Journal of Public Health*, 96, *8*, 1,342-1,346.

Agaku, Israel T., Brian, A. King. & Shanta, R. Dube. (2014). "Current Cigarette Smoking Among Adults — United States, 2005-2012." *Morbidity and Mortality Weekly Report*, 63, *2*, 29-34.

American Academy of Pediatrics. (2012). "Breastfeeding and the Use of Human Milk." *Pediatrics*, 115, *2*, 496-506.

Babcock, Julia C., Sarah, A. Miller. & Cheryl, Siard. (2003). "Toward a Typology of Abusive Women: Differences Between Partner-Only and Generally Violent Women in the Use of Violence." *Psychology of Women Quarterly*, 27, *2*, 153-161.

Bavolek, Stephen J. & Richard, G. Keene. (1999). *Adult-Adolescent Parenting Inventory: AA-PI-2, Assessing High-Risk Parenting Attitudes and Behaviors*. Asheville, NC: Family Development Resources, Inc.

Boller, Kimberly., Deborah, Daro., Patricia Del, Grosso., Russell, Cole., Diane, Paulsell., Bonnie, Hart., Brandon, Coffee-Borden., Debra, Strong., Heather, Zaveri. & Margaret, Hargreaves. (2014). *Making Replication Work: Building Infrastructure to Implement, Scale-Up. & Sustain Evidence-Based Early Childhood Home Visiting Programs with Fidelity*. Princeton, NJ: Mathematica Policy Research.

Brooks-Gunn, Jeanne. & Greg, J. Duncan. (1997). "The Effects of Poverty on Children." *The Future of Children*, 7, *2*, 55-71.

Brooks-Gunn, Jeanne. & Lisa, Markman. (2005). "The Contribution of Parenting to Ethnic and Racial Gaps in School Readiness." *The Future of Children*, 15, *1*, 139-168.

Brown, Brett V. & Sharon, Bzostek. (2003). "Violence in the Lives of Children." *Child Trends Databank: CrossCurrents*, Issue, 1.

Burrell, Lori., Elizabeth McFarlane, S., Darius, Tandon., Loretta, Fuddy., Philip, Leaf. & Anne, K. Duggan. (2009). "Home Visitor Relationship Security: Association with Perceptions of Work, Satisfaction. & Turnover." *Journal of Human Behavior in the Social Environment*, 19, *5*, 592-610.

Campbell, Jacquelyn C. (2002). "Health Consequences of Intimate Partner Violence." *The Lancet*, 359, 9,31*4*, 1,331-1,336.

Carlson, Marcia J. & Katherine, A. Magnuson. (2011). "Low-Income Fathers' Influence on Children." *Annals of the American Academy of Political and Social Science*, 635, *1*, 95-116.

Carroll, Christopher., Malcolm, Patterson., Stephen, Woodrew, Booth., Jo, Rick. & Shashi, Balain. (2007). "A Conceptual Framework for Implementation Fidelity." *Implementation Science*, 2, 40.

Centers for Disease Control and Prevention. (2014a). "Fetal Alcohol Spectrum Disorders (FASDs)." Website: www.cdc.gov/ncbddd/fasd/alcohol-use.html.

Centers for Disease Control and Prevention. 2014b. "Injury Prevention & Control: Adverse Childhood Experiences (ACE) Study." Website: www.cdc.gov/violenceprevention/acestudy.

Chandra, Prasanta C., Henry, J. Schiavello., Bala, Ravi., Alan, G. Weinstein. & Hook, F. B. (2002). "Pregnancy Outcomes in Urban Teenagers." *International Journal of Gynecology and Obstetrics*, 79, *2*, 117-122.

Child and Adolescent Health Measurement Initiative. (2013). "Overview of Adverse Child and Family Experiences Among U.S. Children." Baltimore, MD: Data Resource Center for Child and Adolescent Health. Available at www.childhealthdata.org.

Chittleborough, Catherine R., Debbie, A. Lawlor. & John, W. Lynch. (2011). "Young Maternal Age and Poor Child Development: Predictive Validity from a Birth Cohort." *Pediatrics*, 127, *6*, e1,436-e1,444.

Chomitz, Virginia Rall., Lilian, W., Cheung, Y. & Ellice, Lieberman. (1995). "The Role of Lifestyle in Preventing Low Birth Weight." *The Future of Children*, 5, *1*, 121-138.

Chung, Esther K., Kelly F. McCollum, Irma T. Elo, Helen J. Lee. & Jennifer F. Culhane. (2004). "Maternal Depressive Symptoms and Infant Health Practices Among Low-Income Women." *Pediatrics*, 113, *6*, e523-e529.

Combs-Orme, Terri., Janet, Reis. & Lydia Dantes, Ward. (1985). "Effectiveness of Home Visits by Public Health Nurses in Maternal and Child Health: An Empirical Review." *Public Health Reports*, 100, *5*, 490-499.

Cummings, Mark E. & Patrick, T. Davies. (1994). "Maternal Depression and Child Development." *Journal of Child Psychology and Psychiatry*, 35, *1*, 73-122.

Currie, Janet. & Enrico, Moretti. (2003). "Mother's Education and the Intergenerational Transmission of Human Capital: Evidence from College Openings." *Quarterly Journal of Economics*, 118, *4*, 1,495-1,532.

Davis, Elysia Poggi., Nancy, Snidman., Pathik, D. Wadhwa., Laura, M. Glynn., Chris Dunkel, Schetter. & Curt, A. Sandman. (2004). "Prenatal Maternal Anxiety and Depression Predict Negative Behavioral Reactivity in Infancy." *Infancy*, 6, *3*, 319-331.

Doyle, Orla., Colm, P. Harmon., James, J. Heckman. & Richard, E. Termblay. (2009). "Investing in Early Human Development: Timing and Economic Efficiency." *Economics and Human Biology*, 7, *1*, 1-6.

Dube, Shanta R., Robert F. Anda., Vincent, J. Felitti., Valerie, J. Edwards. & David, F. Williamson. (2002). "Exposure to Abuse, Neglect. & Household Dysfunction Among Adults Who Witnessed Intimate Partner Violence as Children: Implications for Health and Social Services." *Violence and Victims*, 17, *1*, 3-17.

Duggan, Anne., Loretta, Fuddy., Elizabeth, McFarlane., Lori, Burrell., Amy, Windham., Susan, Higman. & Calvin, Sia. (2004). "Evaluating a Statewide Home Visiting Program to Prevent Child Abuse in At-Risk Families of Newborns: Fathers' Participation and Outcomes." *Child Maltreatment*, 9, *1*, 3-17.

Duncan, Greg J. & Jeanne, Brooks-Gunn. (2000). "Family Poverty, Welfare Reform. & Child Development." *Child Development*, 71, *1*, 188-196.

DuPlessis, Helen M., Robert, Bell. & Toni, Richards. (1997). "Adolescent Pregnancy: Understanding the Impact of Age and Race on Outcomes." *Journal of Adolescent Health*, 20, *3*, 187-197.

Durlak, Joseph A. & Emily, P. DuPre. (2008). "Implementation Matters: A Review of Research on the Influence of Implementation on Program Outcomes and the Factors Affecting Implementation." *American Journal of Community Psychology*, 41, 3-*4*, 327-350.

Eamon, Mary Keegan. (2001). "The Effects of Poverty on Children's Socioemotional Development: An Ecological Systems Analysis." *Social Work*, 46, *3*, 256-266.

Early Childhood Development. (2014). "Tribal Maternal, Infant. & Early Childhood Home Visiting." Website: www.acf.hhs.gov/ programs/ ecd/ programs/home-visiting/ tribal-home-visiting.

Eaton, William W., Karen, Neufeld., Li-Shiun, Chen. & Guojun, Cai. (2000). "A Comparison of Self-Report and Clinical Diagnostic Interviews for Depression: Diagnostic Interview Schedule and Schedules for Clinical Assessment in Neuropsychiatry in the Baltimore Epidemiologic Catchment Area Follow-Up." *Archives of General Psychiatry*, 57, *3*, 217-222.

Economic Research Service. 2013a. "Rural-Urban Continuum Codes." Website: www.ers.usda.gov/ data-products/ rural-urban-continuum-codes.aspx.

Economic Research Service. 2013b. "What Is Rural?" Website: www.ers.usda.gov/topics/rural-economy-population/rural-classifications/what-is-rural.aspx.

Egerter, Susan., Paula, Braveman. & Kristen, Marchi. (2002). "Timing of Insurance Coverage and Use of Prenatal Care Among Low-Income Women." *American Journal of Public Health*, 92, *3*, 423-427.

Felitti, Vincent J., Roberta, F. Anda., Dale, Nordenberg., David, F. Williamson., Alison, M. Spitz., Valerie, Edwards., Mary, P. Koss. & James, S. Marks. (1998). "Relationship of Childhood Abuse and Household Dysfunction to Many of the Leading Causes of Death in

Adults: The Adverse Childhood Experiences (ACE) Study." *American Journal of Preventive Medicine*, 14, *4*, 245-258.

Filene, Jill H., Jennifer, W. Kaminski., Linda, Anne Valle. & Patrice, Cachat. (2013). "Components Associated with Home Visiting Program Outcomes: A Meta-Analysis." *Pediatrics*, 132, *2*, S100-S109.

Fixsen, Dean L., Karen, A. Blasé., Sandra, F. Naoom. & Frances, Wallace. (2009). "Core Implementation Components." *Research on Social Work Practice*, 19, *5*, 531-540.

Fixsen, Dean L., Sandra, F. Naoom., Karen, A. Blasé., Robert, M. Friedman. & Frances Wallace. (2005). *Implementation Research: A Synthesis of the Literature*. Tampa, FL: Louis de la Parte Florida Mental Health Institute, National Implementation Research Network.

FRIENDS National Resource Center for Community-Based Child Abuse Prevention. "Continuous Quality Improvement." Website: http://friendsnrc.org/continuous-quality-improvement. Accessed August, 12, 2014.

Gillespie, David F. & Susan, E. Cohen. (1984). "Causes of Worker Burnout." *Children and Youth Services Review*, 6, *2*, 115-124.

Ginsburg, Golda S., Rachel, L. Grover. & Nick, Ialongo. (2005). "Parenting Behaviors Among Anxious and Non-Anxious Mothers: Relation with Concurrent and Long-Term Child Outcomes." *Child and Family Behavior Therapy*, 26, *4*, 23-41.

Glover, Vivette. (2011). "Annual Research Review: Prenatal Stress and the Origins of Psychopathology: An Evolutionary Perspective." *Journal of Child Psychology and Psychiatry*, 52, *4*, 356-367.

Gomby, Deanna S. (2000). "Promise and Limitations of Home Visitation." *JAMA*, 284, *11*, 1,430-1,431.

Gorber, Sarah Connor., Sean, Schofield-Hurwitz., Jill, Hardt., Geneviève, Levasseur. & Mark, Tremblay. (2009). "The Accuracy of Self-Reported Smoking: A Systematic Review of the Relationship Between Self-Reported and Cotinine-Assessed Smoking Status." *Nicotine and Tobacco Research*, 11, *1*, 12-24.

Grote, Veit., Torstein, Vik., Rüdiger, von Kries., Veronica, Luque., Jerzy, Socha., Elvira, Verduci., Clotilde, Carlier. & Berthold, Koletzko. The European Childhood Obesity Trial Study Group. 2010. "Maternal Postnatal Depression and Child Growth: A European Cohort Study." *BMC Pediatrics*, 10, 14.

Hadley, Jack. (2003). "Sicker and Poorer — The Consequences of Being Uninsured: A Review of the Research on the Relationship Between Health

Insurance, Medical Care Use, Health, Work. & Income." *Medical Care and Research and Review*, 60, *2*, 3S-75S.

Harding, Kathryn., Joseph, Galano., Joanne, Martin., Lee, Huntington., & Cynthia, J. Schellenbach. (2007). "Healthy Families America Effectiveness: A Comprehensive Review of Outcomes." *Journal of Prevention and Intervention in the Community*, 34, *1*, 149-179.

Health Resources and Services Administration. (2011). *Affordable Care Act Maternal, Infant. & Early Childhood Home Visiting Program: Supplemental Information Request for the Submission of the Updated State Plan for a State Home Visiting Program*. OMB Control No. 0915-0336. Washington, DC: Health Resources and Services Administration.

Hellmuth, Julianne C., Kristina, Coop Gordon., Gregory, L. Stuart. & Todd, M. Moore. (2013). "Women's Intimate Partner Violence Perpetration During Pregnancy and Postpartum." *Maternal and Child Health Journal*, 17, *8*, 1,405-1,413.

Idler, Ellen L. & Yael, Benyamini. (1997). "Self-Rated Health and Mortality: A Review of Twenty-Seven Community Studies." *Journal of Health and Social Behavior*, 38, *1*, 21-37.

Kaminski, Jennifer Wyatt., Linda, Anne Valle., Jill, H. Filene. & Cynthia, L. Boyle. (2008). "A Meta-Analytic Review of Components Associated with Parent Training Program Effectiveness." *Journal of Abnormal Child Psychology*, 36, *4*, 567-589.

Kohout, Frank J., Lisa, F. Berkman., Denis, A. Evans. & Joan, Cornoni-Huntley. (1993). "Two Shorter Forms of the CES-D Depression Symptoms Index." *Journal of Aging and Health*, 5, *2*, 179-193.

Kroenke, Kurt., Robert, L. Spitzer., Janet, B., Williams. W. & Bernd, Löwe. (2010). "The Patient Health Questionnaire Somatic, Anxiety. & Depressive Symptom Scales: A Systematic Review." *General Hospital Psychiatry*, 32, *4*, 345-359.

Kutty, Nandinee K. (2008). *Using the Making Connections Survey Data to Analyze Housing Mobility and Child Outcomes Among Low-Income Families*. Washington, DC: National Housing Conference, Center for Housing Policy. LeCroy, Craig Winston. & Kate Whitaker. (2005). "Improving the Quality of Home Visitation: An Exploratory Study of Difficult Situations." *Child Abuse and Neglect*, *29*, 1,003-1,013.

Lee, Helen J., Irma, T. Elo., Kelly, F. McCollum. & Jennifer, F. Culhane. (2009). "Racial/Ethnic Differences in Breastfeeding Initiation and Duration Among Low-Income Inner-City Mothers." *Social Science Quarterly*, 90, *5*, 1,251-1,271.

Lemon, Stephenie C., Wendy, Verhoek-Oftedahl. & Edward, F. Donnelly. (2002). "Preventive Healthcare Use, Smoking. & Alcohol Use Among Rhode Island Women Experiencing Intimate Partner Violence." *Journal of Women's Health and Gender-Based Medicine*, 11, *6*, 555-562.

Lillie-Blanton, Marsha. & Catherine, Hoffman. (2005). "The Role of Health Insurance Coverage in Reducing Racial/Ethnic Disparities in Health Care." *Health Affairs*, 24, *2*, 398-408.

Linver, Miriam R., Anne, Martin. & Jeanne, Brooks-Gunn. (2004). "Measuring Infants' Home Environment: The IT-HOME for Infants Between Birth and, 12 Months in Four National Data Sets." *Parenting*, 4, 2-*3*, 115-137.

Lipsky, Sherry., Raul, Caetano., Craig, A. Field. & Shahrzad, Bazargan. (2004). "Violence-Related Injury and Intimate Partner Violence in an Urban Emergency Department." *Journal of Trauma and Acute Care Surgery*, 57, *2*, 352-359.

Livingston, Gretchen. & Vera, Cohn. (2010). *The New Demography of American Motherhood*. Washington, DC: Pew Research Center.

Love, John M., Ellen, Eliason Kisker., Christine, Ross., Helen, Raikes., Jill, Constantine., Kimberly, Boller., Jeanne, Brooks-Gunn., Rachel, Chazan-Cohen., Louisa, Banks Tarullo., Christy, Brady-Smith., Allison, Sidle Fuligni., Peter, Z. Schochet., Diane, Paulsell. & Cheri, Vogel. (2005). "The Effectiveness of Early Head Start for, 3-Year-Old Children and Their Parents: Lessons for Policy and Programs." *Developmental Psychology*, 41, *6*, 885-901.

Magura, Stephen. & Alexandre, B. Laudet. (1996). "Parental Substance Abuse and Child Maltreatment: Review and Implications for Intervention." *Children and Youth Services Review*, 18, *3*, 193-220.

Martin, Joyce A., Brady, E. Hamilton., Stephanie, J. Ventura., Michelle, J., Osterman, K. & Mathews, T. J. (2013). *Births: Final Data for, 2012*. Washington, DC: U.S. Department of Health and Human Services, National Center for Chronic Disease Prevention and Health Promotion, National Center for Health Statistics, National Vital Statistics System.

McDaniel, Marla. & Christopher, Lowenstein. (2013). *Depression in Low-Income Mothers of Young Children: Are They Getting the Treatment They Need?* Washington, DC: The Urban Institute.

McFarlane, Elizabeth., Lori, Burrell., Loretta, Fuddy., Darius, S., Tandon, D., Christian, Derauf., Philip, Leaf. & Anne, Duggan. (2010). "Association of Home Visitors' and Mothers' Attachment Style with Family Engagement." *Journal of Community Psychology*, 38, *5*, 541-556.

McLanahan, Sara. & Marcia, Carlson. (2010). "Fathers in Fragile Families." Pages, 368-396 in Michael E. Lamb (eds.), *The Role of the Father in Child Development*, 5th ed. New York: Wiley & Sons.

Michalopoulos, Charles., Anne, Duggan., Virginia, Knox., Jill, H. Filene., Helen, Lee., Emily, K. Snell., Sarah, Crowne., Erika, Lundquist., Phaedra, S. Corso. & Justin, B. Ingels. (2013). *Revised Design for the Mother and Infant Home Visiting Program Evaluation*. OPRE Report, 2013-18. Washington, DC: U.S. Department of Health and Human Services, Administration for Children and Families, Office of Planning, Research and Evaluation.

Miilunpalo, Seppo., Ilkka, Vuori., Pekka, Oja., Matti, Pasanen. & Helka, Urponen. (1997). "Self-Rated Health Status as a Health Measure: The Predictive Value of Self-Reported Health Status on the Use of Physician Services and on Mortality in the Working-Age Population." *Journal of Clinical Epidemiology*, 50, *5*, 517-528.

Montaño, Daniel E. & Danuta, Kasprzyk. (2008). "Theory of Reasoned Action, Theory of Planned Behavior. & the Integrated Behavior Model." Pages, 67-96 in Karen Glanz, Barbara K. Rimer. & Kasisomayajula Viswanath (eds.), *Health Behavior and Health Education: Theory, Research. & Practice*, 4th ed. San Francisco: John Wiley & Sons.

Mulder, Eduard J. H., Pascale, G. Robles., de Medina, Anja C., Huizink, Bea., Van den Bergh, R. H., Jan, K. Buitelaar. & Gerard, H. A. Visser. (2002). "Prenatal Maternal Stress: Effects on Pregnancy and the (Unborn) Child." *Early Human Development*, 70, 1-*2*, 3-14.

National Institute on Drug Abuse. (2011). "Topics in Brief: Prenatal Exposure to Drugs of Abuse." Website: www.drugabuse.gov/publications/topics-in-brief/prenatal-exposure-to-drugs-abuse.

National Research Council and Institute of Medicine. (2000). *From Neurons to Neighborhoods: The Science of Early Childhood Development*. Washington, DC: National Academy Press.

Noonan, Kelly., Nancy, E. Reichman., Hope, Corman. & Dhaval, Dave. (2007). "Prenatal Drug Use and the Production of Infant Health." *Health Economics*, 16, *4*, 361-384.

Northcote, Jeremy. & Michael, Livingston. (2011). "Accuracy of Self-Reported Drinking: Observational Verification of 'Last Occasion' Drink Estimates of Young Adults." *Alcohol and Alcoholism*, 46, *6*, 709-713.

Patient Protection and Affordable Care Act. (2010). Pub. L. No. 111-148.

Petterson, Stephen M. & Alison, Burke Albers. (2001). "Effects of Poverty and Maternal Depression on Early Child Development." *Child Development*, 72, *6*, 1,794-1,813.

Pollack, Harold., Paula, M. Lantz. & John, G. Frohna. (2000). "Maternal Smoking and Adverse Birth Outcomes Among Singletons and Twins." *American Journal of Public Health*, 90, *3*, 395-400.

Protecting Access to Medicare Act. (2014). Pub. L. No. 113-93.

Raikes, Helen H., Jean Ann, Summers. & Lori, A. Roggman. (2005). "Father Involvement in Early Head Start Programs." *Fathering*, 3, *1*, 29-58.

Reichman, Nancy E. & Deanna, L. Pagnini. (1997). "Maternal Age and Birth Out-comes: Data from New Jersey." *Family Planning Perspectives*, 29, *6*, 268-295.

Reichman, Nancy E., Julien, O. Teitler., Irwin, Garfinkel. & Sara, S. McLanahan. (2001). "Fragile Families: Sample and Design." *Children and Youth Services Review*, 23, 4/*5*, 303-326.

Ross, Lori E. & Linda, M. McLean. (2006). "Anxiety Disorders and During Pregnancy and the Postpartum Period: A Systematic Review." *Journal of Clinical Psychiatry*, 67, *8*, 1,285-1,298.

Rubin, David M., Amanda, L. R., O'Reilly, Xianqun Luan., Dingwei Dai, A., Russell, Localio. & Cindy, W. Christian. (2011). "Variation in Pregnancy Outcomes Following Statewide Implementation of a Prenatal Home Visitation Program." *Archives of Pediatrics and Adolescent Medicine*, 165, *3*, 198-204.

Russell, Marcia., Donna, M. Czarnecki., Richard, Cowan., Elizabeth, McPherson. & Pamela, J. Mudar. (1991). "Measures of Maternal Alcohol Use as Predictors of Development in Early Childhood." *Alcoholism: Clinical and Experimental Research*, 15, *6*, 991-1,000.

Shankaran, Seetha., Barry, M. Lester., Abhik, Das., Charles, R. Bauer., Henrietta, S. Bada., Linda, Lagasse. & Rosemary, Higgins. (2007). "Impact of Maternal Substance Use During Pregnancy on Childhood Outcome." *Seminars in Fetal and Neonatal Medicine*, 12, *2*, 143-150.

Smith, Paige Hall., Jo Anne, L. Earp. & Robert, DeVellis. (1995). "Measuring Battering: Development of the Women's Experience with Battering (WEB) Scale." *Women's Health*, 1, *4*, 273-288.

Sommer, Kristen S., Thomas, L. Whitman., John, G. Borkowski., Dawn, M. Gondoli., Jennifer, Burke., Scott, E. Maxwell. & Keri, Weed. (2000). "Prenatal Maternal Predictors of Cognitive and Emotional Delays in Children of Adolescent Mothers." *Adolescence*, 35, *137*, 87-112.

Spitzer, Robert L., Kurt, Kroenke., Janet, B., Williams, W. & Bernd, Löwe. (2006). "A Brief Measure for Assessing Generalized Anxiety Disorder: The GAD-7." *Archives of Internal Medicine*, 166, *10*, 1,092-1,097.

Staveteig, Sarah. & Alyssa, Wigton. (2000). *Racial and Ethnic Disparities: Key Findings from the National Survey of America's Families*. Washington, DC: The Urban Institute.

Sternberg, Kathleen J., Michael, E. Lamb., Charles, Greenbaum., Dante, Cicchetti., Samia, Dawud., Rosa, Manela Cortes., Orit, Krispin. & Fanny, Lorey. (1993). "Effects of Domestic Violence on Children's Behavior Problems and Depression." *Developmental Psychology*, 29, *1*, 44-52.

Strader, Kathleen., Jacqueline, Counts. & Jill, Filene. (2013). "Federal Home Visiting Under the Affordable Care Act." *Zero to Three*, 33, *3*, 51-57.

Stuart, Gregory L., Todd, M. Moore., Julianne, C. Hellmuth., Susan, E. Ramsey. & Christopher, W. Kahler. (2006). "Reasons for Intimate Partner Violence Perpetration Among Arrested Women. *Violence Against Women*, 12, *7*, 609-621.

Summers, Alicia. (2006). *Children's Exposure to Domestic Violence: A Guide to Research and Resources*. Reno, NV: National Council of Juvenile and Family Court Judges.

Swan, Suzanne C., Laura, J. Gambone., Jennifer, E. Caldwell., Tami, P. Sullivan. & David, L. Snow. (2008). "A Review of Research on Women's Use of Violence with Male Intimate Partners." *Violence and Victims*, 23, *3*, 301-314.

Tajima, Emiko A. (2004). "Correlates of the Co-Occurrence of Wife Abuse and Child Abuse Among a Representative Sample." *Journal of Family Violence*, 19, *6*, 399-410.

Tong, Van T., Patricia, M. Dietz., Brian, Morrow., Denise, V. D'Angelo., Sherry, L. Farr., Karilynn, M. Rockhill. & Lucinda, J. England. (2013). "Trends in Smoking Before, During. & After Pregnancy — Pregnancy Risk Assessment Monitoring System, United States, 40 Sites, 2000-2010. *CDC Surveillance Summaries*, 62, SS*06*, 1-19.

U.S. Department of Health and Human Services. (2004). *The Health Consequences of Smoking: A Report of the Surgeon General*. Atlanta, GA: U.S. Department of Health and Human Services, Centers for Disease Control and Prevention, National Center for Chronic Disease Prevention and Health Promotion, Office on Smoking and Health.

U.S. Department of Health and Human Services. (2009a). *Depression During and After Pregnancy*. Washington, DC: U.S. Department of Health and Human Services, Office on Women's Health.

U.S. Department of Health and Human Services. (2009b). *Head Start Program Performance Standards*. Washington, DC: U.S. Department of Health and Human Services, Administration for Children and Families, Office of Head Start.

Van den, Bergh., Bea, R. H. & Alfons, Marcoen. (2004). "High Antenatal Maternal Anxiety Is Related to ADHD Symptoms, Externalizing Problems. & Anxiety in, 8-and, 9-Year-Olds." *Child Development*, 75, *4*, 1,085-1,097.

Waldfogel, Jane., Terry-Ann, Craigie. & Jeanne, Brooks-Gunn. (2010). "Fragile Families and Child Wellbeing." *The Future of Children*, 20, *2*, 87-112.

Weiss, Heather B. (1993). "Home Visits: Necessary but Not Sufficient." *The Future of Children*, 3, *3*, 113-128.

Weiss, Michael J., Howard, S. Bloom. & Thomas, Brock. (2013). "A Conceptual Framework for Studying the Sources of Variation in Program Effects." *Journal of Policy Analysis and Management*, 33, *3*, 778-808.

Whitaker, Robert C. (2014). "Mindfulness and Workplace Functioning Among Home Visitors in Head Start." Presentation made to the National Summit on Quality in Home Visiting Programs, Washington, DC, January, 29, 2014.

Williams, Jessica R., Reem, M. Ghandour. & Joan, E. Kub. (2008). "Female Perpetration of Violence in Heterosexual Intimate Relationships: Adolescence Through Adulthood." *Trauma Violence Abuse*, 9, *4*, 227-249.

Wilson, Katherine R. & Margot, R. Prior. (2011). "Father Involvement and Child Well-Being." *Journal of Pediatrics and Child Health*, 47, *7*, 405-407.

Wolfe, David A., Claire, V. Crooks., Vivien, Lee., Alexandra, McIntyre-Smith. & Peter, G. Jaffe. (2003). "The Effects of Children's Exposure to Domestic Violence: A Meta-Analysis and Critique." *Clinical Child and Family Psychology Review*, 6, *3*, 171-187.

End Notes

[1] Brooks-Gunn, Jeanne, and Greg J. Duncan, "The Effects of Poverty on Children," *The Future of Children* 7, 2 (1997): 55-71.

[2] National Research Council and Institute of Medicine, *From Neurons to Neighborhoods: The Science of Early Childhood Development* (Washington, DC: National Academy Press, 2000).

[3] Doyle, Orla, Colm P. Harmon, James J. Heckman, and Richard E. Tremblay, "Investing in Early Human Development: Timing and Economic Efficiency," *Economics and Human Biology* 7, 1 (2009): 1-6.

[4] The Protecting Access to Medicare Act of 2014 provided an additional $400 million investment through FY 2015.

[5] The legislation required grantees (states, territories, and tribal entities) to show improvement in six specified benchmark areas. In addition, the legislation required that MIECHV-funded programs be designed to improve individual outcomes for participating families in seven areas. Because there is considerable overlap between the benchmark areas and the individual participant outcomes, this report uses the term "outcomes" to refer to both lists. MIHOPE is designed to assess impacts relevant to all of these outcomes.

[6] To determine which national models were considered evidence-based, HHS commissioned the Home Visiting Evidence of Effectiveness (HomVEE) review. Models met the HHS criteria for evidence of effectiveness if they had at least one study of at least moderate quality with statistically significant impacts in two or more of eight outcome domains, or at least two such studies with statistically significant impacts in the same domain.

[7] Linver, Miriam R., Anne Martin, and Jeanne Brooks-Gunn, "Measuring Infants' Home Environment: the IT-HOME for Infants Between Birth and 12 Months in Four National Data Sets," *Parenting* 4, 2-3 (2004): 115-137.

[8] "Continuous quality improvement" is a process to ensure programs are systematically improving services and increasing positive outcomes for the families they serve. See FRIENDS National Resource Center for Community-Based Child Abuse Prevention, "Continuous Quality Improvement," website: http://friendsnrc.org/continuous-quality-improvement, accessed August 12, 2014.

[9] Brooks-Gunn and Duncan (1997).

[10] National Research Council and Institute of Medicine (2000).

[11] Doyle, Harmon, Heckman, and Tremblay (2009).

[12] Brooks-Gunn and Markman (2005).

[13] Weiss (1993).

[14] Combs-Orme, Reis, and Ward (1985); Harding et al. (2007); Love et al. (2005).

[15] The Protecting Access to Medicare Act of 2014 provided an additional $400 million investment through the middle of fiscal year 2015.

[16] For more information on HomVEE, visit http://homvee.acf.hhs.gov.

[17] The 14 programs were Child FIRST, Early Head Start -Home Based Program Option, Early Intervention Program for Adolescent Mothers, Early Start (New Zealand), Family Check-Up, Healthy Families America, Healthy Steps, Home Instruction for Parents of Preschool Youngsters, Maternal Early Childhood Sustained Home Visiting Program, Nurse-Family Partnership, Oklahoma's Community-Based Family Resource and Support Program, Parents as Teachers, Play and Learning Strategies Infant, and SafeCare Augmented.

[18] Filene, Kaminkski, Valle, and Cachat (2013).

[19] Carroll et al. (2007); Fixsen, Blase, Naoom, and Wallace (2009).

[20] Boller et al. (2014).

[21] The evaluation design is described in detail in Michalopoulos et al. (2013), and briefly summarized here.

[22] The other areas include principles of child health, safety, and nutrition; adult learning principles; and family dynamics.

[23] U.S. Department of Health and Human Services (2009b).

[24] The legislation also included a 3 percent set-aside for grants to tribal entities (which includes tribes, tribal organizations, and urban Indian organizations). Tribal MIECHV grantees were not included in MIHOPE. For more information on Tribal MIECHV see Early Childhood Development (2014).

[25] To determine which home visiting models would be defined as evidence-based, HHS commissioned the Home Visiting Evidence of Effectiveness (HomVEE) review. See http://homvee.acf.hhs.gov.

[26] The analysis that follows includes only states, not territories. Because states used different metrics to measure child maltreatment, child maltreatment indicators are excluded from this cross-state comparison.

[27] HRSA Region 1 includes the six New England states. HRSA Region 2 includes New Jersey and New York. HRSA Region 3 includes Delaware, the District of Columbia, Maryland, Pennsylvania, Virginia, and West Virginia. HRSA Region 4 includes Alabama, Georgia, Florida, Kentucky, Mississippi, North Carolina, South Carolina, and Tennessee. HRSA Region 6 includes Arkansas, Louisiana, New Mexico, Oklahoma, and Texas.

[28] To designate counties as metropolitan or nonmetropolitan, this report follows the Department of Agriculture Economic Research Service's Rural-Urban Continuum Codes classification scheme. See Economic Research Service (2013a).

[29] Health Resources and Services Administration (2011).

[30] The Northeast included New England, New York, Pennsylvania, New Jersey, Delaware, and Maryland.

[31] The South included Virginia, West Virginia, North and South Carolina, Georgia, Florida, Alabama, Mississippi, Louisiana, Tennessee, Kentucky, Arkansas, Texas, and Oklahoma.

[32] The Midwest and Plains region included Ohio, Michigan, Indiana, Illinois, Missouri, Wisconsin, Minnesota, Iowa, North and South Dakota, Nebraska, and Kansas.

[33] The Mountain and West region included California, Oregon, Washington, Hawaii, Alaska, Arizona, Nevada, New Mexico, Colorado, Utah, Idaho, Wyoming, and Montana.

[34] Fixsen et al. (2005); Rubin et al. (2011).

[35] McFarlane et al. (2010).

[36] Burrell et al. (2009); LeCroy and Whitaker (2005); Whitaker (2014).

[37] Boller et al. (2014); Burrell et al. (2009), Whitaker (2014).

[38] It is important to note that MIHOPE families are not necessarily representative of families served by the Maternal, Infant, and Early Childhood Home Visiting Program (MIECHV) because MIHOPE did not include a random sample of local home visiting programs, as discussed in Section 3.

[39] Chandra et al. (2002); DuPlessis, Bell, and Richards (1997); Sommer et al. (2000).

[40] Chittleborough, Lawlor, and Lynch (2011); Reichman and Pagnini (1997).

[41] Abraído-Lanza, Ambrister, Florez, and Aguirre (2006).

[42] Kutty (2008).

[43] The legislation required grantees (states, tribes, and tribal organizations) to show improvement in six specified benchmark areas. In addition, the legislation required that MIECHV-funded programs be designed to improve individual outcomes for participating families in seven areas. Because there is considerable overlap between the benchmark areas and the individual participant outcomes, this report uses the term "outcomes" to refer to both lists. MIHOPE is designed to assess impacts relevant to all of these outcomes.

[44] Idleand Benyamini (1997); Miilunpalo et al. (1997).

[45] U.S. Department of Health and Human Services (2004); National Institute on Drug Abuse (2011); Chomitz, Cheung, and Lieberman (1995); Lemon, Verhoek-Oftedahl, and Donnelly (2002); Magura and udet (1996); Russell et al. (1991); Centers for Disease Control and Prevention (2014a).

[46] Agaku, King, and Dube (2014); Tong et al. (2013).

[47] Tong et al. (2013).

[48] Gorber et al. (2009); Northcote and Livingston (2011).

[49] Chung et al. (2004); Petterson and Albers (2001); Ross and McLean (2006).

[50] Ginsburg, Grover, and Ialongo (2005); Glover (2011); Mulder et al. (2002); Van den Bergh and Marcoen (2004); Davis et al. (2004).

[51] U.S. Department of Health and Human Services (2009a).

[52] McDaniel and Lowenstein (2013).
[53] Chung et al. (2004).
[54] Eaton, Neufeld, Chen, and Cai (2000); Kroenke, Spitzer, Williams, and Löwe (2010).
[55] Hadley (2003).
[56] Egerter, Braveman, and Marchi (2002).
[57] Lillie-Blanton and Hoffman (2005). Even among low-income, nonelderly adults, minorities, particularly Hispanics, are more likely to be uninsured than other groups. Low-income, nonelderly, non-Hispanic black adults are slightly less likely to be insured than their non-Hispanic white counterparts. See Staveteig and Wigton (2000).
[58] Martin et al. (2013).
[59] Carlson and Magnuson (2011); McLanahan and Carlson (2010); Wilson and Prior (2010).
[60] Linver, Martin, and Brooks-Gunn (2004).
[61] American Academy of Pediatrics (2012).
[62] Lee, Elo, McCollum, and Culhane (2009).
[63] Reichman, Teitler, Garfinkel, and McLanahan (2001); Waldfogel, Craigie, and Brooks-Gunn (2010).
[64] Waldfogel, Craigie, and Brooks-Gunn (2010).
[65] Sternberg et al. (1993); Wolfe et al. (2003).
[66] Tajima (2004).
[67] Note that because these measures are self-reported, the results here may underestimate the prevalence of these behaviors.
[68] Hellmuth, Gordon, Stuart, and Moore (2013); Swan et al. (2008); Stuart et al. (2006); Babcock, Miller, and Siard (2003).
[69] Lipsky, Caetano, Field, and Bazargan (2004).
[70] Dube et al. (2002).
[71] Dube et al. (2002); Summers (2006).
[72] Brown and Bzostek (2003).
[73] Duncan and Brooks-Gunn (2000); Aber, Bennett, Conley, and Li (1997); Eamon (2001).
[74] Livingston and Cohn (2010).
[75] Centers for Disease Control and Prevention (2014b); Felitti et al. (1998).
[76] Since the original Adverse Childhood Experiences study, researchers have used various categories to create a cumulative measure of adverse childhood experiences. For example, the National Survey of Children's Health developed a modified list based on its survey, which included the following: (1) perceived socioeconomic hardship; (2) the divorce or separation of parents; (3) the death of a parent; (4) a parent who served time in jail; (5) witnessing domestic violence; (6) being a victim of neighborhood violence; (7) living with someone who was mentally ill, suicidal, or severely depressed; (8) living with someone with an alcohol or drug problem; and (9) one's perception of being treated or judged unfairly due to race or ethnicity. See Child and Adolescent Health Measurement Initiative (2013).
[77] Campbell (2002); Cummings and Davies (1994); Currie and Moretti (2003); Grote et al. (2010); Noonan, Reichman, Corman, and Dave (2007); Pollack, Lantz, and Frohna (2000); Shankaran et al. (2007); U.S. Department of Health and Human Services (2004); Chandra et al. (2002); DuPlessis, Bell, and Richards (1997); Sommer et al. (2000).
[78] Gomby (2000).
[79] Weiss, Bloom, and Brock (2013).
[80] "Continuous quality improvement" is a process to ensure programs are systematically improving services and increasing positive outcomes for the families they serve. See FRIENDS National Resource Center for Community-Based Child Abuse Prevention (2014).
[81] The four national models were also asked for whom they expect programs to assume some responsibility. Early Head Start-Home Based Program Option indicated that programs are expected to assume some responsibility for the mother, biological father, other father figure, and subsequent pregnancies. Healthy Families America indicated that programs are

expected to assume some responsibility for other father figures, a child's other familial caregivers, a mother's other children, and subsequent pregnancies. Parents as Teachers indicated that programs are expected to assume some responsibility for a mother's other children.

[82] Duggan et al. (2004); Raikes, Summers, and Roggman (2005).

[83] The aim related to this outcome is to reduce the frequency with which women have another child within two years.

[84] Strader, Counts, and Filene (2013).

[85] Montaño and Kasprzyk (2008); Durlak and DuPre (2008).

[86] Patient Protection and Affordable Care Act (2010).

[87] Kaminski, Valle, Filene, and Boyle (2008).

[88] Healthy Families America discourages this behavior to avoid potentially traumatizing or disempowering a parent who may not yet be able to get the same reaction from an infant as a home visitor.

[89] Gillespie and Cohen (1984).

[90] Fixsen et al. (2005).

[91] The percentage relating to tobacco use includes women who reported using tobacco within the previous two years and those who reported permitting smoking in the home. The percentage relating to substance use includes women who reported using illegal drugs or binge drinking shortly before pregnancy.

ACCOMPANYING CD-ROM
TABLE OF CONTENTS:

THE MOTHER AND INFANT HOME VISITING PROGRAM EVALUATION: EARLY FINDINGS ON THE MATERNAL, INFANT, AND EARLY CHILDHOOD HOME VISITING PROGRAM [APPENDICES]

Charles Michalopoulos, Helen Lee, Anne Duggan et al.

INDEX

F

G

H

I

K

L

M

N

O

P

Q

R

S

T

U

V

W

Y